More Advance Praise for *Success Under Stress*

"Keep this book handy! Sharon Melnick's tools and techniques really work. Our colleagues saw a truly positive change in their resilience to workplace stressors. Her 'able-to-use-NOW-in-the-stressful-moment' techniques dissipate crowded thoughts, bulging project lists, and hyper-adrenalized physiology. They are powerful and immediately effective."

—Anne Camille Talley
Retired Senior Director of Global Market Research
Professional Development for a major pharmaceutical company

"From the advice in this book, I no longer feel overwhelmed by the growing list of things to do, nor the personalities, politics, or inevitable problems. I now approach situations with a level head and open mind, and come out ahead. No one else knows the secret to why I am successful; they just know that I am a better leader and communicator. I am more satisfied in my contribution and ultimately happier in my life. Read this book! Dr. Melnick is in your corner giving you the tools, power, and confidence to become a better and more effective version of you."

—Elizabeth Lee
Director of Marketing, Pitney Bowes

"Dr. Melnick has a unique gift of raising your perspective on what the true stumbling blocks to success really are, then "lifts you out of the fog" to reach your goals and objectives. In my years of exposure to many in the field of business development coaching, there is no one that stands out from the rest, and is more qualified than Sharon Melnick. Her book, *Success Under Stress,* will awaken the 'Sleeping Giant' within."

—Bruce Libman
President and CEO, Total Network Consulting

"Don't get mad, get results! Sharon Melnick provides practical, holistic tools to help you avoid distracting 'noise' and enables you to convert obstacles to opportunities. Read this book to achieve, and be valued!"

—J. Scott Berniker
a Sales & Market Development Vice President

"Sharon's stress-busting secrets have helped me launch to the next level in my career while creating an amazing home-life balance as well. Read what she says in this book, it will change your life."

—Stacy Francis
President of Francis Financial, Inc.,
and Founder, Savvy Ladies

"Sharon Melnick's presentations at our Working Mother national conferences have been among the highest-rated by our audience of women leaders, and diversity and work-life professionals, and her book is an absolute must-read. *Success Under Stress* contains truly fresh solutions for the challenges of working parents everywhere."

—Janet Wigfield
Executive Director of Conferences+Events,
Working Mother Media

"We face an epidemic of overwhelmed Superwomen—causing hormone chaos, weight gain, and sleeplessness. With this book, at last Dr. Melnick delivers us a prescription for powerful choices that create balance amidst high-achievement and hyperbusy days."

—Sara Gottfried, M.D.
Integrative Physician, author of *The Hormone Cure:
Reclaim Balance, Sleep, Vitality, and Sex Drive
with The Gottfried Protocol*

"As a mother of two and an expat working in Beijing, stress had been part of my day for years. That is, until we learned Dr. Melnick's tools for *Success Under Stress*. They were extremely relevant and useful to better our daily life and career satisfaction. I recommend that women leaders or aspiring leaders learn the skills in this book, especially the ideas of "Be Impeccable for your 50%"; how to influence others, and the breathing techniques."

—Fang Hu
Chemical Engineer, Procter and Gamble

"The tools in this book are invigorating and inspiring—a truly fresh look at common challenges."

—Nora Cashion
Director at a Fortune 100 Company

"In this age of rapid, unrelenting change, resilience is a core competency for sustaining productivity and projecting leadership presence. *Success Under Stress* provides turnkey strategies and cutting-edge techniques for being resilient regardless of external challenges. It is a must-read for men and women in business today."

—Kelley Black
Managing Director, Balancing the Executive Life

"*Success Under Stress* is *the* handbook for anyone who aspires to a full life, which, by definition, will be busy and often stressful! Sharon's easy, and quick-to-implement techniques, combined with her explanations of the physiology underpinning our emotional reactions, have been revelatory for me. Managers, new graduates, business owners, and all those experiencing a professional challenge will find quiet power in the pages of this book. I only wish I'd been able to read it a decade ago!"

—Rebecca Jackson
Startup Advisor/Consultant

"I accomplish so much more now than I ever used to, with far more confidence and significantly less stress. The wealth of information contained in this book also helped me blow past my stuck-in-the-mud sense of powerlessness about not taking a career step to achieve my dreams. If you're feeling stressed-out, overwhelmed, not achieving your goals, or just wish you could be more confident in your life at home or at work, BUY THIS BOOK – IT WILL CHANGE YOUR LIFE!"

—Marti Boylan
artist

"In today's pressure cooker world there is no better book than Success Under Stress for women entrepreneurs. Every woman CEO should buy it! Keep it at your desk. Use it daily, like I do!"

—Eli Davidson
Award-winning author, small business CEO mentor

"Without focus or direction, time and the opportunities it brings can easily get frittered away. Before we know it, we're exhausted or frustrated because we haven't achieved our goals and we're now a year older! *Success Under Stress* is a timely and much needed resource for busy adults who are constantly battling too many demands for their time. Sharon Melnick does a great job of helping us achieve clarity and the ability to practice the wisdom of serenity."

—Helen Whelan
CEO, Success Television

Success
Under Stress

Powerful Tools for Staying Calm,

Confident, and Productive

When the Pressure's On

SHARON MELNICK, PhD

AMACOM

New York • Atlanta • Brussels • Chicago • Mexico City
San Francisco • Shanghai • Tokyo •Washington, D.C.

Bulk discounts available. For details visit:
www.amacombooks.org/go/specialsales
Or contact special sales:
Phone: 800-250-5308
E-mail: specialsls@amanet.org
View all the AMACOM titles at: www.amacombooks.org
American Management Association: www.amanet.org

This publication is designed to provide accurate and authoritative information in regard to the subject matter covered. It is sold with the understanding that the publisher is not engaged in rendering legal, accounting, or other professional service. If legal advice or other expert assistance is required, the services of a competent professional person should be sought.

Library of Congress Cataloging-in-Publication Data

Melnick, Sharon.
    Success under stress : powerful tools for staying calm, confident, and productive
    when the pressure's on / Sharon Melnick.
        p.   cm.
    Includes bibliographical references and index.
    ISBN 978-0-8144-3212-9
    1. Job stress.   2. Stress management.   3. Success in business.   4. Quality of
    work life.   I. Title.
    HF5548.85.M45 2013
    158.7'2—dc23   2012030861

About AMA

American Management Association (www.amanet.org) is a world leader in talent development, advancing the skills of individuals to drive business success. Our mission is to support the goals of individuals and organizations through a complete range of products and services, including classroom and virtual seminars, webcasts, webinars, podcasts, conferences, corporate and government solutions, business books and research. AMA's approach to improving performance combines experiential learning—learning through doing—with opportunities for ongoing professional growth at every step of one's career journey.

Printing number

10 9 8 7 6 5 4 3 2 1

To my parents, Susan and Neil Melnick,
for their generosity

To Dr. Joseph Michael Levry,
for his wisdom

CONTENTS

SECTION I

Constant Stress: Reclaiming the Power to Succeed

SECTION II

Taming the Stress of Too Much to Do and Too Many Obstacles

SECTION III

Solutions for Self-Imposed Stress: How to Care Less About What Other People Think

SECTION IV

Rx for Relationship Stress

SECTION V

Create Success Under Stress All Around You

ACKNOWLEDGMENTS

To Steve Lefkovits for being the first to invite me to speak on your stage and for coining the term "Success Under Stress." To Jackie Green for the insight that American Management Association members would be interested in the topic of resilience to workplace stress and to Dave Summers for your enthusiastic mind and your foresightful introduction to Ellen Kadin. Very genuine thanks to Team SUS at AMACOM: Ellen Kadin for your very supportive communication and expert coordination and to Louis Greenstein for doing a yeoman's job to greatly improve the readability of this manuscript and for your seasoned thoughtfulness and engaging nature.

To Erin Kelly and Elaine Lafferty: Thank you for being there, providing a professional perspective on my foibles as a writer, and providing examples of what a real writer could produce. To Diane O'Connell for keen edits on early drafts and never-ending flexibility. To Rebecca Jackson for parachuting in with a lifebuoy: Thank you for thoughtful and incisive editorial efforts, enthusiastic adoption of the tools, and our ongoing strategic exchange and friendship.

Inexpressible thanks to readers of early chapters for your time and heartfelt input that led to immediate improvements in the manuscript: Jennifer Hartwell, Maria Kadison, and Nancy Stewart. Thank you to the women leaders at Procter & Gamble, GE, Pfizer, and Merck for your appreciative feedback and questions during our trainings—they helped sharpen my thinking and maintain my passion during the deep writing phase of the book. My deep gratitude to all my clients for sharing their stories and allowing me to be a part of their transformation. Some of their stories are told (with identifiers changed) in this book.

Thank you to Ann Pope for her able assistance and dedication to this book and to Oren Shai for his resourcefulness and reliability in the research phase.

The advice in this book was shaped and directly offered by the wisdom of the following experts, who took time from busy lives to share their thought leadership. Genuine thanks go to:

David Allen, Creator of Getting Things Done productivity method
Carol Evans, CEO of Working Mother Media
Keith Ferrazzi, CEO of FerrazziGreenlight, Thought Leader on Professional Relationships
Sara Gottfried, MD, Integrative Medicine Doctor and Hormone Expert
Sheila McCaffrey, Former Director of Strategic Talent Management, Pitney Bowes
Bruce McEwen, PhD, Professor, Rockefeller University
Joel Nigg, PhD, Professor of Psychology at Oregon Health & Science University
Marcelle Pick, OB/GYN NP, Cofounder of Women to Women healthcare clinics
David Rock, Cofounder of NeuroLeadership Institute
Rich Schefren, Founder of Strategic Profits and Business Growth Expert
Monica Worline, PhD, Cofounder of Vervago

My deep gratitude to the following: Kelley Black, founder of Balancing the Executive Life, who prompted the shaping of many of the ideas in this book, for her generous spirit and many layered intelligence. Sonia Sequeira, PhD, Neuroscientist at Memorial Sloan-Kettering Cancer Center and Cofounder of Naam Biomedical Society, for her patient sharing of wisdom about foundations of stress physiology and its antidotes and for the way she graciously serves as my role model. And to Dr. Joseph Michael Levry, founder of Naam Yoga, for his vast knowledge, tireless educational efforts, and vision of a better future.

Thank you to my icons of Success Under Stress for being you a nd sharing your natural talents: Jason Rubinstein, Andrea Hansen, OiYen Lam, Clare Dolan, and Cindy Morgan. Ongoing appreciation goes to my parents, Susan and Neil, for their support and careful reading of the Introduction, which led to many fruitful changes. And a huge special thank you to Louise, for her unwavering encouragement, "veggies," and inspiration in every way.

What This Book Will Do for You

When you're at your best, you get the satisfaction that comes from completing a project or closing a deal. You're respected. You're well compensated for the value you add to people's lives. You feel accomplished, like you've hit your stride. At the end of the day, you have enthusiasm left over for the people and activities you care about most —and even some peace of mind as well. Yet, many of us are running around with too much to do, facing obstacles to progress, and having to deal with stressed-out people.

Welcome to the "New Normal," where all manner of day-to-day stresses can wear you down and make it harder than ever to stay afloat—let alone achieve your next level of success.

You have more control than you think you do. In this book, you'll learn hundreds of strategies that will enable you to succeed quickly, even in the face of the most common stresses, such as interpersonal friction and having too much work but not enough time. This wealth of skills will make you more resilient and put you more in control of each day. You'll have the luxury of time to think, while you work less and ultimately earn more.

As a business psychologist who's trained and coached more than 6,000 people, I've seen that some are surfing the wave of stress—energetically and confidently turning out successful projects—while others are merely surviving. There's a clear skillset that distinguishes one group from the other. You *already* have a treasure trove of tools at your disposal, but you might not know how to access them.

Once you learn the secrets to *Success Under Stress*, watch your stock rise. Indeed, 71% of senior executives around the world reported that the resilience to turn obstacles into opportunities is "very" to "extremely" important in determining whom to retain.[1] Business owners who have a strategic approach to their day see a rapid growth in their business.

I wrote *Success Under Stress* so that you can make your mark on your organization and be the go-to person in your field, without sacrificing quality of life. No longer will challenging events define your day or the business results you get. You will cope better with stresses, but more than that, you'll know how to replace obstacles with opportunities so that you eliminate what's causing the stress. You'll be able to take charge of your workload and cut through complexity to see new ideas that will help you stand out from the pack. You'll know how to motivate and influence others to follow your suggestions (and stop wasting energy on frustration). You'll develop the courage to speak up in meetings and to pursue clients that may seem above your level. Whenever you feel challenged or stuck, you'll have the tools you need to move through the situation and make it go *your way*.

Success Under Stress goes beyond the conventional wisdom of eat right, get enough sleep and, if things get really hectic, "take a deep breath and walk around the block." Many people are finding these approaches helpful, but insufficient for the way modern-day demands interfere with their achievement and quality of life. This book will show you how to approach any challenging situation by:

- **Changing Your Perspective.** A new point of view helps find new solutions.

- **Changing Your Physiology.** Get focused when you're over-whelmed, energized when you're exhausted, and calm when you're wired or frustrated.
- **Changing the Problem.** Solve your stresses at the root cause and you won't have to face them again!

From the very first time you use any one of the tools in this book, you'll notice an immediate decrease in stress and an increase in effectiveness. And when you use tools from *all three* of these approaches you'll be able to turn around any challenging situation.

Best of all: Because I know how busy you are, almost every one of the tools in this book can be learned and implemented in *three minutes or less*. And what will you get?

- **More control in your life.** You will go from an experience of "running around" to thinking clearly and accomplishing intended results. You'll feel more in control of your schedule. You'll be able to reduce the stress of living in fear that you'll overlook important work or miss out on client opportunities. You'll achieve this by making use of your greatest talents. You'll clear away what's been draining your time and energy; you'll be able to say "no" to the tasks and projects that don't hit your "sweet spot."
- **Steady energy and enthusiasm left over at the end of the day.** In this book, you will find tools that enable you to be "On" and "Off" at will. That means you can focus when you need to, and yet also relax when you want to, so you can rejuvenate, enjoy yourself, and sleep through the night. You'll achieve the balance of high-quality work and a satisfying life, minus the internal self-induced pressure to please everybody. If you're prone to beating yourself up, if you think you're not as good as your counterparts, or if you take things too personally, you'll learn how to get back to a positive outlook and positive energy. If you fear speaking up in a meeting or you're reluctant to pick up the phone and call a prospect you think won't want to hear from you, you'll have the

confidence you need to "go for it." If you have to deal with someone who aggravates you, you'll know how to calm your frustration and redirect the situation toward a good resolution. You
will know how to take the emotion out of situations and prevent
reactions that drain you.

- **Opportunities out of obstacles.** You'll learn how to solve problems and dissipate stress—by adjusting when, for example, priorities change or when someone doesn't respond to your request.
You'll learn a mindset and skill set that will thrive in this time of
flux. You'll discover how to "tolerate—even enjoy—recalibrating
careers, business models, and assumptions."[2] Soon, you'll see
emerging trends and get out of your comfort zone while you're
still ahead of the curve. Or, if you feel "stuck" in your circumstances, seeing only the obstacles—production delays, lack of
advancement opportunities, the inability to achieve your financial
goals—you will learn how to turn these situations around and
create success from them.

This book is for you if you:
- Work in an overwhelming environment where you have to in-
fluence people to get things done.
- Own your own business where you "wear all the hats."
- Seek to ease your financial stress and feel you're stretched thin.
- Face a lack of self-confidence that causes you to "get in your own
way" or are reactive in relationships (especially with difficult people).

Here's the game plan to provide you with the tools for Success Under
Stress.

Section I is about reclaiming your power to succeed in the New Normal.

Chapter 1: From Survival Under Stress to Success Under Stress

You will discover how you get caught up in the stress of your day, and how easy it is have an experience in which you feel on top of situations.

Chapter 2: Controlling What You Can Control: The 50% Rule

There is only one rule you need to follow to dramatically increase productivity and goal achievement—and decrease stress. You will learn it in this chapter.

Section II is about stress caused by too much to do and too many obstacles.

Chapter 3: Changing Obstacles to Opportunities

Shift your days away from a bombardment of other people's demands and toward the results you desire. Learn how to turn obstacles into opportunities. Maintain a positive outlook and progress on your personal goals, but also learn healthy detachment if you must remain in a stressful work environment.

Chapter 4: Get the Calm and Focus of a Yoga Class in 3 Minutes (or Less) During Busy Work Days

Learn the secret to higher performance and creative problem solving: it's the ability to have clear focus and all-day energy, balanced with the ability to wind down and rejuvenate on demand. You will learn how to achieve the calm and mental clarity you get from a 90-minute yoga class in three minutes or less while at your desk. And you'll learn how to get back to sleep in three minutes if you wake up worrying about work at night. Be present at work when you are at work, and be present at home when you are at home. Enjoy time away from work without feeling guilty.

Chapter 5: Strategies to Reduce Overload When Everything Is a Priority

Reduce the inflow of requests to which you must respond and make faster progress on projects. Choose the right things to work on and focus on them without letting anything fall through the cracks—even while getting pulled in many directions. Be even more effective—get things done right the first time, get results from your meetings, and solve problems more quickly. Though you still have to contend with the 24/7 demands for your attention, you will be the one to decide when you are available—and you will earn others' respect in the process.

Section III is about learning not to fear what other people think and tackling self-imposed stress.

Chapter 6: The Fastest Way to Build Confidence

Do you seek other people's approval, live in fear of how you'll be judged, procrastinate, or fear to ask for the promotion, raise, or professional fees you deserve? Stop wasting your time and energy. Instead, get on the fast track to self-assurance.

Chapter 7: Quick Fixes to Eliminate Anxiety

Need a shot of confidence? Get anxious before presentations? No problem. You'll learn all about an "inner pharmacy" you can access instantly. Also learn how to reverse trends in your stress system so you can get back your fearlessness and focus.

Chapter 8: Techniques for Turning Self-Criticism into Self-Confidence

You'll learn to trust your own judgment and make decisions swiftly (without agonizing). And, you'll learn how to apply your new-found confidence to move past perfectionism and procrastination. At last, you'll know how to "get out of your own way!"

Section IV is about how to handle relationship stress.

Chapter 9: How to Stay Rational When Someone Is Driving You Nuts

Do you take things too personally? You will learn practical tools to stay calm and poised instead of reacting or saying things you may later regret. No longer will you be hijacked and stressed out by difficult people. You'll always be the person in the room who is respected for staying factual and showing leadership.

Chapter 10: Shift Instantly from Anger to a Cool Head

Learn how to stay cool, calm, and collected even when dealing with someone who makes you seethe with anger, frustration, and impatience (and, even more magically, you'll learn how to calm the other person as well.) Yes, you can use it at home with your kids! You will learn how to clear the build up of negative emotions.

Chapter 11: How to Get Other People to Stop Stressing You Out

What's the next best thing to having a remote control button to make people act the way you want them to? To be able to impact and influence other people's behavior so things get done faster and smoother. You'll know exactly how to approach someone who isn't delivering, and how to influence him or her to meet deadlines on time with no mistakes.

Section V is about how to create Success Under Stress all around you.

Chapter 12: A New Perspective on Balancing Your Work and Life

Expand your definition of work–life balance beyond the number of hours you spend at and away from the office. See that as you have balance within your day and in your own reactions to stress, you will have greater balance in your overall work and life. Learn strategies that are working in the current times to achieve greater control over choices for work–life effectiveness.

Chapter 13: Call to Action: Getting Others to Own Their 50%

As you experience Success Under Stress, you can stop other people from stressing out and raise the game of the people you work and live with. That is the way to create a culture you want to be a part of, whether it's on your team, in your organization, or in your family.

Each strategy in this book will help you lift yourself beyond circumstances that you're just trying to survive—and step up to be more effective in your group; an innovator and *intrapreneur* within your organization; and a leader in your field, your network, and your community. Don't wait for others to approve of you. Don't wait for things to change before you can feel less stressed. Simply use the strategies in this book to achieve *Success Under Stress*.

Constant Stress:
Reclaiming the Power to Succeed

Think you're the only one stressing out? If so, "listen in" on two of my phone conversations and see if you relate to others who are also feeling the heat.

"I've never admitted this to anyone before," Stacy told me. "I can't do it anymore. In fact, sometimes I don't even want to."

Stacy is a mid-career working mother who heads up an internal client service team. When she called me for a consultation, she explained, "There's enormous pressure to get a mounting pile of projects done without a mistake. I know I expect too much of myself, but I'm nervous about lowering my standards. My assistant keeps making mistakes, and I'm worried she'll make a major one that affects our clients. I don't sleep well. I wake up in the middle of the night. Then I have a short fuse. I've snapped at my kids more than a few times lately, and I always feel guilty about it."

I could hear the desperation in Stacy's voice. She had trouble prioritizing because of her frenetic pace and the daily changing priorities. She was operating "in the weeds," trying to do it all herself. A perfectionist, she felt personally responsible for getting everything right. Though exhausted, she kept pushing herself.

We cleaned up Stacy's challenges in a matter of weeks! First, I gave her a technique to get back to sleep within three minutes so she could wake up rested. Next, we prioritized the 61 projects on her plate. As she learned to question herself less and get more done, she felt she had accomplished enough at the end of each day to go home. She learned the tools to push herself when needed and to relax and be present with her family when desired. As a result, her life became more balanced. After she learned communication techniques to minimize her assistant's mistakes, Stacy's relief was visible. As these skills gave her more of a sense of control, we were able to deal with that self-critical "voice" and go over how to stop overreacting with her kids. At home, her guilt began to melt away and, at work, she grew into her potential as a leader. Four months later, Stacy was promoted.

Dan, who owns a financial planning business, told me, "I have tremendous financial goals, and I'm not reaching them. I'm fed up chasing the minnows—I want to land the whale clients like the other guys do. I feel I need to work all the time. I can't miss out on opportunities to get clients, so I don't have the quality of life I work so hard for. Every morning I come to the office with a plan, but then I get interrupted and my plan goes down the drain. On top of it all, my former business partner is being a pain in the neck."

Because Dan lost sight of the big picture, he wasn't getting the most important things done. He'd go home frustrated and come in the next day only to spin his wheels again. A lack of confidence held him back from going for the whale clients. He was frustrated, anxious, and financially stressed.

Dan was ready to break through to the next level of success. We sculpted his business around his considerable talent and identified his unique value to those whale clients. He became clear about where he was headed and what daily critical actions would get him there. As he developed a system for powering down the piles of paperwork, his stress began to subside, and he was able to think straight again. That's when we taught him strategies to put him on the fast track to that "quiet confidence" he wanted when entering a room. Within a month, he was meeting with the whales. And within three months, he landed the biggest deal of his professional career. He ended his business partnership on amicable terms, spent more time with his new wife and—at long last—enjoyed the quality of life for which he'd work so hard!

Are you feeling like Stacy or Dan—pushing hard every day just to stay caught up, but not getting ahead? Are you working hard but not achieving the financial reward or the quality of life you want? Or are you making progress, but at great cost to you and your family?

If so, you can learn a better way, quickly. Channeling stress properly turns coal into diamonds. In later chapters, you'll learn about all the tools (and more) Stacy used to get promoted and Dan used to land a whale client. If you've been handling things well in the New Normal, you'll now be able to do so with less wear and tear. If you've been struggling, you'll pick up a toolkit to put you in control. Like Stacy and Dan, as you apply the skills, you will have greater career satisfaction, improved work-life balance, and better financial security. You'll live life more on your own terms, not just react to it.

1

From Survival Under Stress
to Success Under Stress

Imagine a person who responds to daily challenges and minor emergencies by thinking only of short-term solutions instead of looking at what's best for the future. Unable to see new approaches or new opportunities, he looks only to the past for solutions. He focuses on the problem, not the whole picture. He overreacts; he stresses over how a situation could possibly go wrong, keeping himself anxious and on guard.

If you had such an employee, you wouldn't look to him or her for innovations, would you? And in fact, that employee might not last long with you. Yet, what I just described is a typical stress-system response, left unchecked. Without knowing it, our response to daily stressful events may keep us stuck handling challenges the same way, day after day, thereby preventing us from reaching our next level of success. Clearly, if we don't do something proactively to achieve *Success Under Stress*, we might never have it.

Of course, we want better control over how we respond—we want to respond thoughtfully, not reactively. And, in a manner that's future oriented. We want to build value for a long-term benefit—not just for ourselves, but for everyone we work with as well. We want to respond with the best available option to solve problems, maintain good relationships and conserve energy. That's a Success Under Stress response! One client described his transformation from a typical stress response to one he could control as, "It's like I was driving a clunky car that doesn't turn well, and now I've stepped into a Porsche; my performance is just superior."

Let's get even more specific about the experience you could have when you are more in control of your response to challenging events throughout the day. We'll begin with an example. Here is the "Before" scenario:

It's 4 PM and you are at your desk. It's been a busy day, but the end is in sight. You and your spouse are due to meet at your 11-year-old daughter's end-of-the-year school play in two hours. Your boss calls you into her inner sanctum. Crisis. The president of your division is considering a strategic change, which would pull key resources away from your group. Your boss needs you to put together a 10-minute slide presentation on your big project for a meeting with the president and senior management tomorrow morning at 9 AM. You're not exactly sure what she wants, but you begin to feel overwhelmed, so you decide to leave her office and get started immediately.

On the way back to your desk, your thoughts are scattered: If the number of people on your team were reduced, would you be included? You tell yourself, "Don't go there!" But you sense a hint of panic setting in. You can feel your heart thumping. You imagine what tomorrow's meeting will be like. Why does the president want to hear from *you*? What if you make a mistake or say something that the president thinks is mundane? You get a pit in your stomach. You recall that your boss met with the president a week ago, so you wonder why she's only telling you about this now. You feel resentful, causing your jaw to clench and your neck muscles to tighten.

You feel pressured to get the presentation done now because if you miss your daughter's play you will be inducted into the Bad Parent Hall of Fame. Instinctively, you know you'll get it done somehow, but you expect it will be stressful. Worse yet, you don't know if you'll be proud of what you produce. You feel completely trapped!

You sit down at your desk and try to brainstorm, but you experience tunnel vision. You keep having the same ideas over and over; it's hard to focus. You're racking your brain trying to remember where you filed that presentation your colleague did at the kick-off meeting so you can reference it. But you're running out of time. So you tell yourself to go with the first idea you had, which is to describe the project and its milestones.

Just as you begin to build a little momentum, someone who works for you pops in to hand you a report. You give it a glance and notice the numbers in the last column are off. That means you're going to have to take some time to re-explain it to him. You think about your packed schedule. When will you even have time to review it again? You feel crunched. Your voice has a tone of exasperation as you give him feedback.

You finish a draft, and then rush to your daughter's play, arriving with a minute to spare. It takes so long to settle in that you aren't really present until the second act. That night, you sleep restlessly, worrying about the presentation. In the morning, you're nervous as you enter the meeting, still unsure if you'll deliver exactly what your boss wants. Your presentation goes without a hitch, but you get peppered with a lot of tough questions about the go-forward strategy. You feel intimidated, so you avoid speaking up, even when you have something important to say. After the meeting you soldier on, but feel rattled for the rest of the day. When you pass your boss in the hallway you're anxious whether she'll say anything about it.

In this scenario, your response to stress is a series of interlocking effects, each compounding the one before it. A physical reaction to stress leads to panicked and scattered thoughts. It limits your ability to see the best solutions and interferes with your best judgment. When you don't perform at your best, you chip away at your confi-

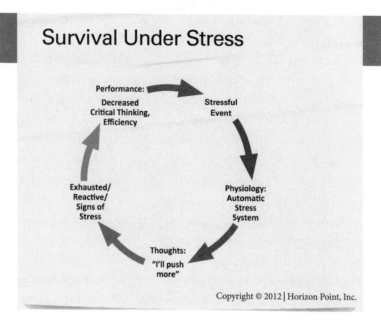

Figure 1.1

dence and put more pressure on yourself in subsequent situations. As depicted in Figure 1.1, your thoughts, your physiology and your responses to the problem form a vicious cycle that I call *Survival Under Stress.*

The stressors that set Survival Under Stress in motion are infinite: When priorities change. When someone gets competitive with you. When your income is lower than expected. When you don't get feedback after your presentation and wonder if "no news is good news." It certainly is going on once your email inbox climbs up to an impossible number. As Ned Hallowell describes it in his seminal article, "Overloaded Circuits": "The sufferer doesn't experience a single crisis but rather a . . . never-ending drip of situations perceived as minor crises. Feeling trapped and wanting to live up to your own and others' expectations of you, you 'suck it up' and don't complain as the workload increases or the results don't appear. Your attitude is one of

'I'll try harder.' You feel a constant low level of panic and guilt. Facing a tidal wave of tasks, the executive becomes increasingly hurried, curt, peremptory and unfocused, while pretending that everything is fine. . . . You've become so used to being in this state of frenzy that you may not recognize that your coping mechanisms aren't working."[1] If you've had any moments recently where the onslaught of demands became so great that you thought to yourself, "Stop the train, I want to get off," now you know why.

Does this cycle remind you of how you respond to stressful situations? Judging from the number of times I've presented the idea of the survival cycle to businesspeople and heard back, "It's like you are in my head," it's certainly the pattern that characterizes many of those with whom you work and live.

Let's return to your 4 PM scenario with the boss. This time you will see the possibility you have to create Success Under Stress. Notice that in this scenario, little time is wasted. The emotional churn barely exists. And, the presentation you draft has more impact on your future and your team's.

In your boss' office, you start by taking a deep breath so you can actually listen closely to her request. You have the presence of mind to ask a few questions to help clarify her needs. You think through a few ways of drafting the presentation and ask your boss if she agrees with you: "It might be better to give a brief overview of the project," you say, "but then focus on the strategic value and bottom line recommendations to improve it going forward. Do you agree?" Yes, she agrees. As you walk back to your office, this clarity enables you to begin forming a mental outline of the presentation.

Back at your desk, you use a one-to-three minute mental reset technique so you can be in the right frame of mind to think clearly and creatively (Chapter 4). You forgive your boss for giving you the assignment at the last minute, and you realize she asked you because she has confidence in you (Chapter 9). You experience a few seconds of nervousness at the thought of presenting in front of the company president. But you know how to use the "Panic Reset" button, an acupressure point that reduces anxiety within seconds (more on this in Chapter 7).

In the brief time remaining, your concentration is steady. Each slide you complete gives you a sense of satisfaction and momentum. You put together a solid presentation—pleased to have a say in your team's future and confident that you'll do a good enough job in the morning. When your assistant pops in to hand you the report, you notice the mistakes. Instead of snapping, you think about the best strategy to influence him to give you the right work. You refer to the recent conversation in which he agreed to take responsibility for his mistakes and fix them, so your conversation is more of a brief touch base to get him on track (Chapter 11).

You arrive at your daughter's play on time, and you beam with pride throughout her performance. After you fall asleep that night, you wake up once but know how to get back to sleep within three minutes (Chapter 4). You arrive at work rested and take a few minutes to review your slides. The presentation goes smoothly and, when there is opportunity to add additional value to the discussion, you speak up without a script (Chapter 6). The president is a woman of few words but you don't necessarily need her explicit praise—you could read her body language and also know inside of you that your presentation was well received. You are on a small high for the rest of the day.

In this scenario, you created a positive spiral—a virtuous cycle. You handled it well from the beginning by preventing your stress response from spiraling out of control. You had constructive and confident thoughts. You were motivated by the last-minute circumstances. In fact, the heightened pressure brought out your best qualities. You achieved a better result, all from small shifts you made in your physiology, your perspective and your approach to the problem. This scenario characterizes *Success Under Stress* (see Figure 1.2).

Many of us are locked into Survival Under Stress but don't even realize it! Lack of sleep, muscle tension, and impaired concentra-

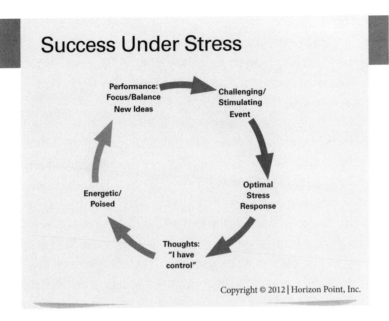

Figure 1.2

tion are often viewed as justifiable by-products of doing business in today's world. Some people see these as badges of honor for being a road warrior and a multitasker. But we might not notice that our decisions aren't based on listening intently or thinking through the facts. We may rush into what is right for the moment—or not act at all - instead of doing what's best for the long term.

And who can blame us? First, consider the sheer volume of demands that require our attention. The average business professional has between 30 and 100 projects on his or her plate—all at once[2]; is interrupted on average seven times per hour[3]; and faces incoming communication from multiple technologies 24 hours a day. You may be paid to think, but it's hard to find the time!

Second, this daily onslaught comes at you against a backdrop of rapid local and global changes that force you to adjust your priorities and innovate to capture the attention of your target market—whether that's your customers, donors, or manager. If you don't keep up the pace, you might not be seen as a contender or you might let a critical item fall through the cracks. You worry that if you don't work all the time you could lose an important client or won't earn enough money. You run mental movies of what might happen if you lose your job or don't earn enough each month.

Third, for many of us, this overload is just the base of a stack of other stresses that compound one another to magnify the effect. For example, perhaps your high expectations of yourself (and others) create an extra layer of pressure to do more. If you have any doubts about yourself, you may worry about what other people think; you may feel the need to invest extra effort in getting their approval. We constantly judge ourselves on whether we are doing enough at work or at home. And yet we know that in order to succeed, it's more important than ever to speak up and show confidence instead of staying in our comfort zone.

In the face of all this, you try to produce meaningful work, make your mark, and be well paid for your services. No wonder stress has become a national epidemic! (Over 80% of workers feel stress on the job[4] and over 70% of healthcare provider visits are due to stress-related conditions.[5]) The pace feels unsustainable, and many of us are already near a breaking point, with no relief in sight.

The New Normal is here to stay, but there's good news: it can work for you. What if you had the ability to complete projects and handle people as smoothly as in the second 4 PM scenario? What if you could be present at work, and present at home? What if you could get off the Survival Under Stress cycle and onto Success Under Stress? In Chapter 2 you'll learn how to do so—and quickly—by flipping the control switch.

Are You on the Survival Under Stress Cycle?

If you want to take a temperature check to understand how much of your life is defined by Survival Under Stress, then take a brief detour and fill out the chart below. You'll feel a sense of accomplishment as you begin to shift to Success Under Stress.

Rate yourself on each of the domains listed on the survey. The higher you rate the item, the more you are displaying the signs of Survival Under Stress. The lower you rate the item, the more you are displaying the signs of Success Under Stress. What are your main sources of stress? Do they have to do with Too Much Work? Self-Confidence? Relationship Friction? After you complete the survey, total your score and see for yourself how much the signs of stress are influencing your effectiveness and happiness.

To what extent are you on the Survival Under Stress cycle? Find out here:

1. Concentration and Focus

1	2	3	4	5	6	7	8	9	10
O	O	O	O	O	O	O	O	O	O

Focus and concentrate well

Racing thoughts/hard time concentrating/a lot of info coming in and head feels like it will explode

2. Quality of Thinking

1	2	3	4	5	6	7	8	9	10
O	O	O	O	O	O	O	O	O	O

Thinking is sharp/See all options/ Think creatively/See opportunities in obstacles/See the big picture

Mind is foggy/Forgetful, short-term memory off/ Get tunnel vision/Get locked into details and overfocus on problem

3. Productivity

1	2	3	4	5	6	7	8	9	10
O	O	O	O	O	O	O	O	O	O

Productive/Organized/ Clear about role and business strategy

Could be more efficient/ Come to work with a plan but end day in frustration after having been distracted

4. Energy level

O   O   O   O   O   O   O   O   O   O
1   2   3   4   5   6   7   8   9   10

Energetic throughout
the day and evening

Wired and/or Tired/Crash
in the afternoon or at end of
day/Go home and numb out
in front of TV

5. Workload

O   O   O   O   O   O   O   O   O   O
1   2   3   4   5   6   7   8   9   10

Workload is stimulating
and challenging
but manageable/
Proactively communicate
to manage expectations

Workload is excessive, over-
whelming/Feel buried/Don't
feel in control of workload/
Wearing too many hats,
stretched thin

6. Body Symptoms

O   O   O   O   O   O   O   O   O   O
1   2   3   4   5   6   7   8   9   10

Relatively free of
Tension/Appetites
are healthy

Muscle aches/Grind teeth/
Headaches/Desires are
reduced/Dark circles under
the eyes

7. On and Off Time

O   O   O   O   O   O   O   O   O   O
1   2   3   4   5   6   7   8   9   10

Rest and renew
regularly/Availability
to others is my choice

Always "on" and checking
phone, text, email (feel
"addicted"/Worried I will
miss out or disappoint
expectations if not always
on)

8. Sleeping

1	2	3	4	5	6	7	8	9	10
○	○	○	○	○	○	○	○	○	○

Wake up rested

Trouble falling asleep/Wake up in middle of the night or early morning and hard to get back to sleep/Sleep through the night but wake up tired

9. Health

1	2	3	4	5	6	7	8	9	10
○	○	○	○	○	○	○	○	○	○

Relatively healthy/
Body absorbs nutrients

Get sick a lot (flu, colds)/Digestive issues/Difficult to gain or lose weight/Salt or sugar cravings

10. Work-Life Balance

1	2	3	4	5	6	7	8	9	10
○	○	○	○	○	○	○	○	○	○

Carved out a workable, satisfying work-life balance/ Have proactively sought solutions /Have peace of mind about choices for now

Still struggle, not at peace/ Feel guilty about making decisions/Feel guilty about house not cleaned/Feel trapped

11. Fearlessness

1	2	3	4	5	6	7	8	9	10
○	○	○	○	○	○	○	○	○	○

Fearless

Live in fear of what others think/Anxious—obsess about or rehash situations that happened or might happen/Focus on worst-case scenarios

12. **Self-Confidence**

1	2	3	4	5	6	7	8	9	10
O	O	O	O	O	O	O	O	O	O

Project Confidence/
Secure

Doubt myself/Self-critical,
beat myself up/Perfectionist—
have standards too high to live
up to for myself (or others)/
Have to do everything, and do
it well

13. **Motivation**

1	2	3	4	5	6	7	8	9	10
O	O	O	O	O	O	O	O	O	O

Motivated and positive
outlook/Take action to
control stress

Feel trapped in circumstances/
Hopeless/Reduced feeling of
joy/Withdraw from social in-
teractions/Disengaged at work

14. **Reactivity**

1	2	3	4	5	6	7	8	9	10
O	O	O	O	O	O	O	O	O	O

Poised, think rationally/
Stay cool, calm,
collected/Thoughtful
before responding/Handle
interruptions with ease

Snap at people (professionally
and personally)/Feel angry,
irritable/Take things personally

15. **Interpersonal Influence**

1	2	3	4	5	6	7	8	9	10
O	O	O	O	O	O	O	O	O	O

Ease in relationships/Know
how to move others to action/
Have gained cooperation of
difficult people

Frustrated/Don't feel heard/
Come home at night talking
about a person who aggravates
me/Wish others would change

16. Relationship Friction

○	○	○	○	○	○	○	○	○	○
1	2	3	4	5	6	7	8	9	10

Comfortable communicating in difficult relationships/ Don't expect the person to change so am not chronically frustrated/Have gained cooperation of difficult people

Someone in my life who is difficult to deal with and causes me a lot of stress/Come home at night talking about this person who aggravates you (or bring the stress of the personal relationship to work)/Feel victimized/Keep hoping it will change, but don't act

17. Coping

○	○	○	○	○	○	○	○	○	○
1	2	3	4	5	6	7	8	9	10

Have a regular practice of healthy coping mechanisms/ Know how to manage myself to stay in a good state

Use alcohol or drugs, take pills to sleep/Stress-related eating/ Don't cope well

On how many items did you rate yourself 5 or higher? That's how much Survival Under Stress characterizes your life. It will be helpful if you identify a few early warning signs so you can take swift measures to prevent the response from getting worse and keeping you in the cycle. What are the canaries in your coal mine? What signs foreshadow that your stress could get out of hand? A typical early warning sign is the first time we say to ourselves, "I don't have time to go to the gym this week." Another is when we say something such as, "I'll just stay up later to get it all done." Or maybe it's the negative tone we use when talking with someone.

Write down the early warning signs of your stress. Then, you can be on the lookout for ways to reverse the trend at an earlier stage in the process.

My early warning signs that I'm on the Survival Under Stress cycle:

_____

_____

_____

_____

_____

2

Controlling What You Can Control:
The 50% Rule

"There's only one corner of the universe you can be certain of improving, and that's your own self"

—ALDOUS HUXLEY

Stress is not necessarily the result of the workload, the lack of response, the interruptions, or the "traffic jam" of unfinished projects and overextended commitments. It occurs when the demands of a situation exceed your perceived ability to control them. The key is that the more you perceive you can control, the lower your stress, and vice versa.

Stress is not external. It's internal. It's not the 100th email of the morning in your inbox per se. You feel overwhelmed because you process that event as, "Mayday, Mayday! I am overloaded." If that email announces a delay in the approval for your project or gives you negative feedback about your proposal, you experience stress from your visceral reaction of worry about your future reputation, job security, and income. If that email is littered with mistakes from your assistant, stress comes from the anger you experience over your inability to control his actions.

As suggested in Chapter 1, we don't generally choose these reactions. Many are hardwired in our brains.[1] And on a moment-to-moment basis, our brains coordinate an elaborate and delicate symphony of responses that will determine our neurochemistry and, consequently, how we feel and what we are prone to think. Without knowing it, once these internal patterns are established, we lock into them. (No worries! You'll learn how to "unlock" in Chapter 4.)

Since stress is experienced internally, changing it is within your control. How to begin? By changing your response.

You can flip an internal "control switch" to take you out of survival mode and into success mode in any situation. All it requires is some proactive effort to steer your responses away from the automatic, involuntary, and reactive toward the deliberate and purposeful.

When you control a situation, you influence the outcome. Each and every time you exercise control—for example, by changing a thought, slowing your breath, choosing your words carefully, or blocking time on your schedule—you determine what happens in your brain, your body, and the situation itself. In a confident and calm state, you work faster, solve problems more easily, and make fewer mistakes. You react more positively to others and can motivate them to help you get desired results.

Any single action can begin to put you on the Success Under Stress cycle. Every time you take control of something you actually can control, you reinforce the other affirmative acts, which keeps you on the positive spiral. Like a butterfly flapping its wings and eventually changing the world, you can create immediate and dramatic shifts in your effectiveness and stress level by exerting control in small situations throughout the day.

Of course, you've been around the block. You may already know you're supposed to "control only what you can control." But are you aware of all that's actually within your control? Are you accessing your control switch consistently—especially in the heat of the moment?

Control What You Can Control

Every challenge can be divided into two categories—the 50% of factors we can control and the 50% we can't (see Figure 2.1). Factors we

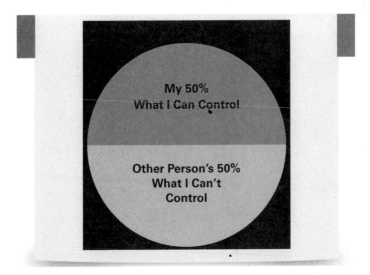

Figure 2.1

can't control include macrolevel forces, such as market trends, technology developments, senior leadership decisions, reorganizations, traffic jams, other people's illnesses, and foreign country bankruptcies. Additionally, there are a myriad of microlevel forces we can't control, such as someone else's tone of voice or what they write in an email.

Things that are out of your control attract your attention like a magnet attracts metal. However, by focusing on factors outside of your control, you're setting yourself up for stress. You're back on the treadmill, merely surviving.

Let's begin by dividing the situation into what's within your control and what's beyond it. Think of a current situation that's stressful for you. In the circle in Figure 2.2, list what's within your control, and what isn't.

Next, focus your internal lens on the matters that are within your control.

When caught in the grips of a stressful moment, remember to focus on what's in your control. To help you do that, I've developed

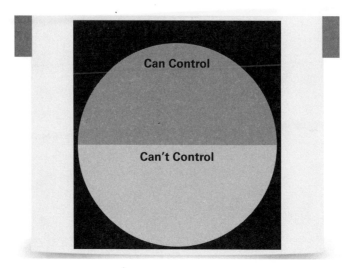

Figure 2.2

a Golden Rule of Resilience that thousands of corporate managers and business owners have used to lift themselves into Success Under Stress in any interaction.

I call it the 50% rule.

Be Impeccable for Your 50%

Being impeccable means controlling only what you can control and taking 100% responsibility for it. By following this rule, you ensure that your contribution is effective before allowing any waste of time, energy, or attention on "the other 50%" that isn't within your control. The 50% rule puts you in charge.

Being impeccable for your 50% motivates you to be proactive. Don't wait for conditions or other people to change. Instead, take charge of the part you can play. Changing your own emotional and physical state allows you to be "part of the solution rather than part of the problem." To illustrate, here are three examples "ripped from the headlines" of my life over the last week.

First, a new client, Vikki is a VP in a large healthcare organization. Her manager is a "screamer," who often would lash out at Vikki.

Stressful! Not in her control! In response, Vikki would become overly talkative to defend the actions for which she was being reprimanded. She began to dread those meetings and felt frazzled for hours after she left them.

Vikki learned to be impeccable for her 50%: She used the breathing technique you will learn in Chapter 10 to stay cool, calm, and collected in the face of her manager's outbursts. She prepared and rehearsed her talking points ahead of the meeting so she could refer to them concisely in the heat of the moment—and she gave thought to aligning her proposals with her boss's specific motivations (as you will learn in Chapter 11). She managed to keep in mind that her boss was unable to handle her own emotions and that the "screaming" had nothing to do with Vikki's competence. Now when she met with her boss she was confident and effective. Within a few weeks, Vikki persuaded her boss to follow her recommendations for a large-scale reorganization. In fact, she was ultimately put in charge of the merged divisions! In short, she didn't try to change her boss; she changed her own perspective, physiology, and approach to the problem. That's the 50% rule at work!

Second, earlier this week I emailed someone at a company who'd hired me to conduct a training session for its high potentials. I needed a response by the end of the week, but it didn't arrive. Have you ever been in that frustrating situation? I wanted to scream or barge into the person's office and demand a response!

So, what did I do instead? I challenged my initial reaction of blaming the nonresponder. I didn't know what happened on the other end to cause the delay, but I gave the person the benefit of the doubt. That immediately began to dampen my frustration. I used a breathing technique you will learn in Chapter 4 to help me problem solve so I could think through other options. I got out of the tunnel vision that made me think the email recipient was the only person who could help me resolve the issue. Surely someone else in the organization could provide me with the relevant information.

I also considered whether I had done something to delay the response. I scanned the email to see if I had used effective influencing strategies and if there was anything I could have communicated better. Was I clear regarding the required response? Was my message compelling? And did I align it with the company's interests so management would be motivated to respond promptly?

With all of these active self-management efforts, my attention was diverted into positive action. I had a game plan that made me feel in control. I was steady and able to think clearly for my next client appointment. (Then of course, just to be impeccable for my 50%, I immediately reached out to people who'd contacted me but to whom I hadn't yet replied!)

Third, after conducting a webinar for Women in Cable and Telecommunications, I got a call from Danielle, an attendee. When I asked her how she had applied the tools she learned in the webinar, she said that the night of the training she had a little tiff with her husband and, of course, was tempted to go to sleep angry with him. We laughed as she told me how she remembered the 50% rule *after* she was sarcastic to her husband: "You know, I could have talked to him differently. It really wasn't all him." Once Danielle realized that, she apologized for how she had handled it and gave her feedback respectfully. In return, he offered a mutually agreeable solution to the conflict. They both went to work the next day feeling connected, absent the friction that otherwise would have set them off on the wrong foot.

When you focus on your 50%, you start from the premise that there is always something you can do to shift the situation - even if it doesn't feel that way initially. Keep in mind that there are three categories of stress shifters. No matter what the situation, you can always:

- **Change your perspective**
- **Change your physiology, and**
- **Do something to change the problem**

Even the mere *perception* of control reduces the stimulation of a stress response and will break the Survival Under Stress cycle. This shift in your emotional and physical state will motivate you to want to deal with situations rather than endure them unhappily or avoid them. Literally even a simple, one-minute visualization about how you could bring value to the situation will flood you with positive emotions and alleviate fear. After working with more than 6,000 individuals, I have yet to be told about a "stuck" or stressful situation in which we couldn't identify a handful of things the person could do within seconds, minutes, or days to radically reduce the stress, feel more in control, and create a better outcome.

At this juncture, I should be clear that I'm not encouraging you to control everything you can just for the sake of doing so. Being impeccable means **not** trying to control what is going on "across the line" in other people's 50%. Nor am I advising you to be a control freak who bulldozes over people to get your way. The approach I'm suggesting is meant to be used in the service of a positive intention and help you be less stressed and more effective as you progress toward a worthy goal. The idea is for you to have awareness of your own approaches and other people's styles in order to remove friction and resistance, and get to a solution quicker. Just think of a time that you felt productive and on a roll. You probably had a sense that you were "in control," right?

Q: What if I am impeccable for my 50%, but others aren't for theirs?

A: That's a legitimate question! In fact, I sent my dearest friend an early version of this chapter and the next day she texted me about her school age son and daughter, Mae and Kyle: "My kids were arguing all morning. At a quiet moment I pulled my daughter aside and told her to try the 50% concept in the book. She replied, 'That's a book Kyle should read!'"

I know each of you has a "Kyle" in your life: "I do really good work, but my boss doesn't support me." "I give referrals to other people, but they don't refer back." Here's my response to help you stay on track with this approach: First, being impeccable for your 50% doesn't mean you should give other people a free pass on bad behavior. You want to be impeccable for your 50% because it helps you. It's the only route for keeping stress in check and creating successful outcomes. Being impeccable for your 50% is like the proverbial scenario on the playground in which the other child hits you first, but the teacher only sees your reaction. Your actions alone are all that matter in determining both your reputation and the results you get in your life. When your track record is reviewed, all that will matter is what you did.

Second, part of what you will learn in this book is how to sort through what's within your control and what isn't when it comes to other people. No doubt, you can cite colorful examples of people who don't deliver on time, who exhibit negative attitudes, who are unsupportive, unreliable, indecisive—or worse. You wish you had the remote control button to make them act differently to support your own (or your business's or family's) goals. You want to remember that people are driven by their own biology and psychological background. Through their actions, they reveal their capacity (or lack thereof) to give you what you need.

Following the 50% rule approach brings great clarity to difficult relationships. As a general rule, start by doing everything you can within your own control to improve the situation. Try to make your efforts effective (more on this in Sections III and IV). People often try ineffective strategies for a long time and then conclude that nothing can change. If, after you have been impeccable for your 50%, no change has occurred in the environment or the relationship, you may then conclude that the other person or the situation is currently incapable of change. This gives you information that will help you choose either to continue or to seek another situation. Often, our continued efforts once we pass this point are what make a situation or relationship chronically stressful. That's self-imposed stress!

In most (though not all) situations, truth prevails. A person who is not being impeccable for his 50% faces consequences at some point.

From a spiritual point of view, you might not know the larger scheme of things. Maybe that person will get his due down the line. Maybe he's already suffered hardship you don't know about. But that's not for you to control or worry about. Your task is to be effective under the given conditions or to change yourself or your conditions.

Q: What are the benefits of being impeccable?

A: It may seem like a lot of work, but once you get the hang of it, it will usually take no more than a few seconds or minutes to be impeccable for your 50% in any situation. With a little practice, this approach will become second nature and effortless. You don't have to be "perfect"; you just have to try your best to be intentional.

And the benefits far outweigh the efforts. In each instance where you are impeccable for your 50%, you instantaneously reduce your stress level and get on the path toward the result you want. This approach gives you a lot of power. It builds others' trust in you because it builds your credibility. By the time you've been in an organization or a business network for a while, people know your reputation: whether you're true to your word; whether you deliver on your promises; whether you give or only take, and so on. If you're generally impeccable for your 50 percent, people know to trust your perspective when conflicts arise.

Further, a longstanding body of research shows that people who attribute their successes and failures to their own behaviors and actions are more likely to take proactive steps, while people who believe that external forces such as luck or fate determine their life may lose hope in the face of a stressful situation.[2]

The ability to put yourself into optimal mental and physical states and to bounce back when you get derailed gives you the power to make your best contribution every day. Your colleagues and managers will notice. Your clients and networking partners will notice. Each time you choose (and have the skills) not to react negatively under pressure, you build stronger relationships and are respected. And, of course, an invaluable benefit is that you can walk away from any interaction feeling proud of yourself rather than questioning what the other person thinks about you. All the signs point to the same conclusion: If you want to stay calm, confident, and productive when the pressure's on, you must control what you can control.

Your Ideal Day

Practice having an intention by performing what I call the "Ideal Day" exercise. It helps you gain clarity on how you want to spend time and what you want the quality of your experience to be. First, write down what an ideal work day would look like. For example, what would you do (or not do). What would you have time for and what kinds of things would you accomplish (or not accomplish). How would you describe your feelings, and your experience. Be as detailed as you can. If you're like most people, your Ideal Day will be pretty close to the picture of the way things will be when you are "in control" by following the 50% rule.

Next, write down what your typical day actually looks like. Then, compare the two. Most people have an eye-opening revelation about the gap between their current day and their Ideal Day. For example, a common theme among many participants in my training on resilience is how much built-in time the Ideal Day would include for "thinking" and "reflection," as compared with their current days, which were comprised of back-to-back meetings in different locations. They saw a stark difference between their current day and Ideal Day. As a result, they were able to restructure their days to have time to reflect. This enabled them to do work they are uniquely qualified to do and, therefore, made them better leaders and business owners.

_____

_____

_____

Post your Ideal Day description up on your wall. Revisit and update it as needed. Your Ideal Day is the antidote to the out-of-control aspects of your current day. A clear picture enables you to act intentionally in the interest of creating that Ideal Day. This doesn't mean that people will suddenly stop interrupting you or crises will no longer erupt. Nor does it mean that you'll stop having too much to do. But by following the techniques in the rest of this book, you will know how to take control of your 50% and steer yourself toward your Ideal Day.

In sum, the 50% rule changes your experience from one in which events happen to you to one in which you are in charge. It's a reminder not to survive a stressful situation by waiting for it to change. Instead, take initiative and make yourself feel better. Make your own contribution effective and others will follow.

ACTION PLAN

- Think of a current challenging or stressful situation you face. Using Figure 2.2, write down a list that divides the the situation into those aspects you can control, and those you can't. Focus rigorously on the 50% that you can control and make a list of action steps you can take today or this week.
- Take 3 minutes and write down your vision of your Ideal Day. Include how you spend your time, what you think about, what you accomplish, how you feel during the day and how you interact with others. Post that description where you can refer to it often. Start acting with intention to create that Ideal Day as often as possible.

POINTS TO REMEMBER

- You can flip your internal "control switch" in any moment from automatic, reactive, and involuntary responses to ones that are within your control. Every time you make an effort, however small, you will change the course of the stress you face. You'll immediately feel better. The problem will either be resolved or be easier to manage.

- Every stressful or challenging situation you face can be divided into those aspects that you can control and those you can't. Focus rigorously and take action on the former.

- The 50% rule (**"Be Impeccable for your 50%"**) is the approach that leads to Success Under Stress. Following this rule dramatically decreases stress and increases performance.

- Follow the 50% rule even when others don't. Regardless of their behavior, your actions determine your success and energy level. The benefits of the 50% rule—credibility and trust, confidence, and the ability to switch off the Survival Under Stress cycle and switch on the Success Under Stress cycle—far outweigh the efforts.

- Once you've articulated a desired outcome for a situation, or for your day, you can act intentionally to bring it about. The Ideal Day exercise helps you define a positive intention for the day so you can act in the service of it.

SECTION II

Taming the Stress
of Too Much to Do
and Too Many Obstacles

In the New Normal, we simply have to accomplish more, but with fewer resources. I hear it every day from my training seminar participants:

- "As sales representatives, we have 12 hours of work to do in an eight-hour day."
- "In my telecommunications company, they play the *"and"* game. That's when you have to do that *and* that *and* that. I have to give my all to completing projects *and* network with an eye on my next account *and* find quality time to spend with my family."
- "I'm overwhelmed. I am in meetings much of the day and can't finish what I'm accountable for. I have to be creative and strategic, but I'm just putting out fires all day."

You start your day with a well intended to-do list and end it with memories of interruptions, minor crises, derailments, and "I Need It Now!"

requests. Despite lamenting our 24/7 culture as much as the next person, you're "always on." Priorities, including your own, change frequently. You regularly face that "crunch" moment when everything seems to require your urgent attention and it feels like you're headed for a crash.

In the New Normal, old markets shrink and new trends emerge. These days, many people are staying in their jobs or their industries because they feel stuck, so it may be harder to progress in your organization. Similarly, many people have left their industry to become independent consultants, so your field may be more crowded than ever. If so, it's tough to distinguish yourself to prospective clients—not to mention that your quotas or goals may be higher than ever!

Section II is about how to have more control over daily challenges. You will learn how to **change your perspective** so that you rise to the occasion of dealing with challenging circumstances rather than allowing them to overwhelm you. You will learn mindsets and skill sets that turn obstacles into opportunities and enable you to adjust to changes. Then you will learn how to **change your physiology** so you can have energy when you want it and relaxation when you need it. Finally, you'll learn to **change the problem**. We'll cover strategies for efficiency and effectiveness, aimed at bringing your workload to a manageable level. And you'll learn how to eliminate most interruptions and have more choice over when you're available to other people.

3

Changing Obstacles to Opportunities

"The people who get on in this world are those who look for the circumstances they want, and, if they can't find them, make them."
—GEORGE BERNARD SHAW

The thrashing airplane took its passengers on a series of hair-raising dips. The pilot's voice over the loudspeaker said nothing more alarming than, "Sorry folks, we're experiencing a little more turbulence than usual." The older woman across the aisle from me was turning green. I clutched at the armrests, trying to remember to breathe. And, then, there was the school-age boy a few rows behind us. He shouted with glee as the plane mounted and dropped. He threw his hands up in the air and exclaimed, "Wheeee!" with the exhilaration of riding on a roller coaster.

One event, but three distinct experiences. Why? Conventional wisdom says it's not what happens, but what you make of what happens that matters most. Though you might not be aware of it, you automatically evaluate every situation. Will it enhance or threaten your well-being? Can you take any actions to prevent harm or to achieve benefit? Can you handle it or not? These "appraisals" determine how you will act. Perceive a threat and you will try to protect yourself. Perceive a challenge and you will marshal energy to master it. Conclude that nothing can be done and you will feel trapped and resigned.

Neuroscientists have estimated that human beings experience about 60,000 thoughts during our waking hours each day.[1] No wonder we sometimes feel like our heads are about to explode! In this chapter, you'll learn how to steer those 60,000 thoughts toward a positive outlook and create momentum for your Ideal Day.

In seminal research asking 300 people to record their thoughts about work-day events, Harvard Business School professors Teresa M. Amabile and Steven J. Kramer were able to describe how these thoughts form a running scroll of perceptions, emotions, and motivations regarding what's happening in our external and internal worlds. The researchers' pithy summation is, "Every moment you are performing your job you are working 'under the influence' of your inner work life."[2]

The best way to take control of your own inner work life is to drive all your thoughts in one direction. This is known as *thinking in service of an intention.* **To be intentional, you should have a picture of the kind of outcome you want to create, and then think, feel, and act with purpose toward it.** When you have clear intention, it orients your thoughts to the aspects of the situation you can control. Here are three ways to set an intention and orient your inner work life away from survival mode and toward the cycle of success.

1. Come to Work on Your Own Terms

How would you like to come to work on your own terms instead of feeling subject to the whims of other people? "Sounds good," you may say, "and next, you're going to try and sell me a Bridge to Nowhere, right?" Before you dismiss the idea, remember that you are the instrument of your own success. An important step in achieving any goal is to become the "you" who can think, feel, and act in accordance with reaching that goal. I call this reaching your "Horizon Point." Imagine you are captain of a ship. A captain's job is to train her sights on the destination and keep steering the ship with moment-to-moment course corrections toward that point. Out on the high seas, there will be stormy waves, icebergs, and other ships. The captain can't control any of that, but she can control herself. She can remain steady and agile as she steers the ship around the obstacles and keeps focused on the destination.

The idea of your Horizon Point is to impose a sense of purpose and control on your day. If your purpose is to display the qualities and attributes required for success, it's less likely you'll default into merely reacting to requests and problems thrown your way. No matter what challenge you face, you can always control how you respond to it.

Try this practical approach: As you go through your day, instead of concentrating only on your tasks or appointments, bring more of your attention inward. Think about who you need to be to reach your Horizon Point. This shift in focus will ensure that despite moment-to-moment ups and downs, you're always progressing toward the result you desire. Who do you need to be in order to achieve success? Keep that—your Horizon Point—in mind and you'll maximize your chance of getting there.

Your Horizon Point has a dual role: internal guidance system and filter. There's a bundle of fibers in your brain called the "reticular activating system" (RAS). In part, it's responsible for sorting out which information you want to focus on and which you don't. A clear intention allows your RAS to allow in stimuli you want and filter out stimuli you don't want. Once you have defined who you need to be, you can go through your day being **intentional.** Each moment, each interaction, each meeting, you have a choice: you can act consciously and proactively toward your Horizon Point, or you can let the experience happen to you. As you are about to take an action, you may even want to ask yourself, "Will this help me reach my Horizon Point, or not?"

Finding Your Horizon Point: Exercise 1

Start by listing the qualities, attributes, and skills that make up who you want to be, as well as those that your employer or clients expect you to have. **Your Horizon Point should be the convergence of what**

you want for yourself and what your work requires of you. You might not know what your own bigger picture goals are. That's OK. Your Horizon Point is less about the external goals you want for yourself (such as income level or your next job) and more about who you need to be to achieve that outcome.

Remember Stacy and Dan, my clients from Chapter 1? Perfectionist Stacy had to get everything right, even at the cost of her work-life balance. And Dan wanted to land whale clients instead of minnows, he had trouble realizing his financial goals. Here's how they identified their Horizon Points.

DAN'S HORIZON POINT

As a financial planner, he needed and wanted to be:

* Respected*
* Fearless
* Communicative

* Personable
* Technically proficient
* A skilled salesman

STACY'S HORIZON POINT

As a mid-career head of an internal services team who was told she should stay "out of the weeds," Stacy wanted to:

* Be respected
* Have a seat at the table
* Delegate effectively
* Be Caring but firm
* Think strategically

* Enjoy time off and be present for her family
* Be Confident, not so hard on herself, take things less seriously

Now, you try the exercise. The more specific you are about exactly what qualities and skills describe who you need to be, the more

---

* Notice that Dan said he wanted to be respected. The problem is, no one can control other people's respect, and Horizon Points are all about what we *can* control. So we refined Dan's description to " have *self*-respect" or "be worthy of other's respect."

likely you'll remember to be it! The ship's captain doesn't take out the map to start figuring out where she wants to go after the 20-foot waves hit. She has a clear destination ahead of time. The more clear you are upfront, the easier it is to check in with yourself and know whether or not you're on course toward being that person. What qualities and attributes do you want at your Horizon Point?

_____

_____

_____

_____

Finding Your Horizon Point: Exercise 2

If you took the first exercise seriously, you probably listed a minimum of five qualities and attributes that, when achieved, will lead you to have the success you want. In order to make this easy to refer to in the moment—and more likely to cut to your very essence—you need a way of encapsulating that list into a concise phrase, image, or a tangible feeling in your body. This is your Horizon Point. Here are some examples.

PAMELA'S HORIZON POINT

Pamela was a junior partner at a Big Four consulting firm who wanted to become a senior leader. But she was getting derailed, spending too many hours providing drawn-out responses to technical emails from clients and colleagues—and she always had an extra long to-do list of tedious administrative tasks. She worried constantly about how others judged her. Was she acting in the service of that Horizon Point each day? No! Here's a glimpse of who Pamela wanted to be at her Horizon Point:

- Know her value, and share strategic insights more with C-suite clients
- Be a great mentor and coach to the people on her team
- Not stress about what other people think of her
- Have time to train for a bike fundraiser

She decided to use the phrase **"Confident Leader"** to encapsulate her Horizon Point. She began to make time in her day to prepare strategic advice for her C-suite meetings. She mentored her team members to take over the email monitoring functions, and she became more intentional about how she spent her personal time. Meanwhile, she asked for assignments that gave her more exposure to senior leaders. Six months later, she was promoted to the head of the regional office. Nine months after that, she was assigned to an international decision-making committee. That summer she finished her first 100-mile bike race. All because she started to think and act like who she wanted to be at her Horizon Point.

Carl's Horizon Point

Carl was the head of a small insurance firm. He wanted to:

- Be productive, and "ahead" in his day—making sales calls before 10:00 AM
- Get home early to tend his garden and spend time with his new wife
- Be a powerful provider - move with confidence from one meeting to another and be a mentor for his sales representatives

He made his encapsulating phrase **"I'm the Man!"** When he said it or thought about it, his whole face and posture exuded energy. (Soon after working with Carl, I gave his example in a training session with real estate agents. We all laughed when one of the women raised her hand to say, "*I* want to be the Man!" Each of you can find your own version of the Man!) Carl began thinking of himself as, and acting like, "the Man!" He came into work early, made his sales calls before 9:30, and saw himself as deserving a seat at the table with his A-level clients. He grew his business by 80% within nine months.

JEANINE'S HORIZON POINT

Jeanine was the head of production at a fashion company. She had a short fuse. When her direct reports asked her questions, she'd snap at them, intolerant of their mistakes. She didn't sleep well at night, and (no surprise) her team had high turnover. She wanted to maintain her high standards while effectively coaching and mentoring her team members; she also wanted to be calmer and sleep at night.

Jeanine's encapsulating phrase was: **"I'm the Chief Problem-Solving Officer."** From that point on, when her staff came to her with question or mistakes, she welcomed them. After all, helping them solve their problems was her job. Employee retention improved on her team, and the CEO recognized her for her role in generating the highest profits in the company's history for six months straight.

Have another look over your list of qualities and attributes and behaviors. Is there an image or phrase that comes to mind? Be creative, and have fun with it. Try to make the essence of your Horizon Point something that inspires and motivates you. Spend a little time on this (and don't worry; it can always evolve over time) because all of the other strategies in this book are intended to help you be *that* person when the going gets tough. Make it your purpose each workday to act in accordance with your Horizon Point. Especially in the middle of situations that could derail you or set you up to act counterproductively, remember how you defined who you want to be. How would (IMAGINE YOUR ENCAPSULATING PHRASE HERE) handle this situation?

What is your Horizon Point's encapsulating phrase?

_____

_____

You can't always control your manager's shifting priorities, the reorganization in the pipeline, whether prospects will return your call, or when you'll meet the person who helps you land your next job or deal. But you *can* control what you think, the actions you take, and how you overcome your own fears or inefficiencies. Even just calling up the phrase or image or feeling of your Horizon Point breaks the Survival Under Stress cycle by shifting your attention away from external stresses you can't control toward your own purpose.

Keep your phrase and the image it conveys to you front and center with reminder pictures, post-it notes, or screen savers, and by repeating your statement throughout the day.

Here's how Dan and Stacy cut through complexity and challenges to reach their goals faster by setting an intention to think, feel, and act toward their Horizon Points.

Dan's Horizon Point

Dan wanted to be a fearless, respected, communicative, skilled salesman. His Horizon Point was "**Fearless Guide.**" He stopped looking at those big whale clients as wealthy prospects who wouldn't want to do business with a "small fry." Instead, he focused on the value he could bring as a highly competent provider, offering customized, thoughtful advice at a lower cost than at the big firms. He didn't wait for them to respect him. Instead, he learned to respect himself and soon he was asking for those meetings (Fearless). He improved his "sales pitch" by making it more about educating the prospect (being a Guide). He put together possible scenarios and financial models that piqued their interest. That's how he won their massive accounts!

Stacy's Horizon Point

For her Horizon Point, Stacy wanted to stay at the "**Top of the Mountain.**" It was a visual that reminded her of times she had been happy at the top of the mountain on vacation. She could see all the things going on in the valley, yet not be involved in the details. This image would remind her to focus on the larger strategic goals instead of re-acting automatically to the workflow in front of her. She didn't have to do it all herself. With this approach, she had an idea to reorganize the teams in her group. Her boss approved her proposed plan, and she became the senior strategic head of the whole group.

Who do you want to be at your Horizon Point?

_____

_____

_____

2. Turn Obstacles into Opportunity

We've just discussed how you can focus on an intention you have for yourself as a way of organizing and overcoming the myriad demands you face daily. Another way to change your perspective is to learn how to see an obstacle as something you can turn into an opportunity. This skill is now widely considered a "core competency"—at the crux of what most employees and leaders are asked to do as companies operate in rapidly changing industries. Business owners who can turn obstacles into opportunities will keep their operations afloat and their staff on board.

An excellent (though outdated) example of seeing opportunity was told in Benjamin Zander's delightful book, *The Art of Possibility*.[3] Two shoe salesmen are sent to Africa. After checking out the territory, one telegrams the home office, "No one in Africa wears shoes. I'm coming home." The other salesman telegrams, "No one in Africa wears shoes. Send the whole sales team!" Where one salesman saw an obstacle, another saw an opportunity.

Recently, as a member of the Advisory Board of the non-profit Foundation for Social Change and the coach of its fearless CEO, Louise Guido, I had a front-row seat to watch this agility in action. The

Foundation developed a curriculum to teach life skills and business basics to young women and girls in developing countries. Despite a partnership with the United Nations and early successes in creating path-changing outcomes for children, the Foundation faced funding challenges. Initially, CEO Guido tried multiple pathways for possible donors, from individuals to large companies (because that was the way non-profits were accustomed to raising funds.) She began to grow frustrated. She was getting "too close" to the situation and locked into the Survival Under Stress cycle.

As she was on the brink of discontinuing the Foundation, we discussed how she could take a step back and re-frame the funding challenge as an opportunity instead of an obstacle. She decided to start a "for-benefit enterprise" that would fund and sustain the non-profit. Within six months, the Foundation developed a mobile application and tablet-based version of its curriculum. She flew around the world and inked partnership deals with companies wanting to reach this "bottom-of-the-pyramid" demographic and by micropayments made by the mobile users themselves when they download the apps. These micropayments may be pennies on the dollar, but when you have 200+ million users, they add up! Now the Foundation is funded, millions of people around the world receive beneficial education, and large companies "do well by doing good."

Here's an approach to turning a work-related obstacle into an opportunity that can be helpful if you feel trapped in your current work situation. Maybe you are in a role that doesn't have apparent advancement opportunities. Maybe you believe that it's harder than ever to earn a bonus or get an equally well-rewarded position elsewhere. Or, maybe you tell yourself that you've been trained to provide a certain kind of service and you can't just leave the field and start over now.

Feeling trapped adds an extra layer to your day-to-day stresses. Instead of concentrating on the negative, entrapping aspects of the situation and complaining about it, remember: **You have choices, even when it seems that you don't.** One way to break the loop is to try turning the situation on its head—maybe even asking, "What's in it for me?"

Lemia, a consumer products salesperson, followed up with me after a training session at her company. Because of a merger, she'd recently begun reporting to a new sales manager from another company. Lemia told me, "I have a six-year track record of stellar performance. The targets we have to hit in order to earn commissions are now harder, so we are not earning the same bonuses we once did. A lot of my personal time is consumed by thinking about work. Last year was my first opportunity for a promotion, but it went to someone from the same company as the sales manager. It's hard when your manager doesn't see the value you bring. Even though I used to be an athlete, I've gained 30 pounds. I am too tired or stressed out to exercise, I'm not saving energy for myself."

Instead of further indulging the feeling that she is subject to unfair and unsatisfying conditions, Lemia turned her situation on its head. She found ways to use her company instead of feeling used by them! She set a goal that was important to her: "For the next six months I will focus on my health, reduce my weight, and generally take care of myself," she said. "Staying at my company allows me to keep a stable position that will enable my goals. I know the systems. I am provided with a company car so I don't have the added expense of a car loan." In short, Lemia realized that as long as she continued to deliver results, her employer would continue to fund her. Meanwhile she can focus on her priorities. She started an early morning regular workout in her home. She began fixing healthy meals to take with her on the road.

Finally, Lemia should be impeccable for her 50% and do the thinking that will lead to clarity of action. Has she created or taken advantage of any opportunities to talk to her boss' boss about her goals? Has she designated her "lines in the sand" and made a commitment to change her situation if those lines are crossed? (Is her line in the sand defined as three more months without discussions about promotion? Six months? Has she already crossed her lines?) This way she knows where she stands and exactly what and when she needs to do something about it.

Four weeks after I suggested she start to "come to work on her own terms," Lemia told me, "I'm reclaiming my life. Now I complete a full and focused day's work instead of spending out-of-control hours that were burning me out, and I start the day consistently with my workout. I have so much more energy and had one of my best months in terms of revenue. It's made a big difference." She realized what was in it for her if she remained at her job for the time being and worked it a different way. By realizing what she stood to gain personally, she was able to change her perspective and re-motivate herself. She approached what looked like a professional obstacle as a personal opportunity—and created a win-win situation for and her employer. Within three months she was promoted.

What's a current obstacle or situation in which you feel stuck? Jot down three ideas you now have about how you can turn that obstacle into an opportunity for you and/or your business.

_____

_____

_____

Q: How can I keep a positive outlook and be happy in the midst of what I see as negative changes in my organization?

A: Good for you for wanting to maintain a positive outlook when conditions are in flux. Change can sometimes be perceived as a threat to everything you've worked for, especially when you don't know what's going to happen. When figuring out how to make sense of change, your stress response system might divert to biased thinking to protect you and to save energy. Your thinking will generally be biased toward negative forecasting—trying to predict worst-case scenarios so you can arm yourself against them.

Perhaps you jump straight to being terminated and then homeless, living under a bridge, without thinking through the 1,000 possible actions you could take before any such eventualities unfold.

When you're confronted with change in your organization, remind yourself to adhere to the 50% rule. It's tempting to comment negatively on other people's decisions or to be fearful of the uncertainty, but the way to stay productive is by managing *yourself*. Try following these steps to **WIN at Change** in your organization:

1. **W**ritten Inventory—Make a three-column chart—your Written Inventory. In the first column, write the implications of the change for your role and for you personally. In the second column, write your personal reactions to each of these implications.

2. **I**ndividual Responsibility—In the third column, write what you personally can do to take responsibility for dealing with the implication and reaction. What can you do to change your perspective and embrace the changes? How can you reprioritize your efforts? How can you be proactive to control what you can control? What are all the actions you can take? Define what you can do to take individual responsibility and be impeccable for your 50%. You may even want to raise this issue with colleagues you trust. Together, go through the exercise about "what you can control."

3. **N**ew Learning Plan—On a separate page, put together your New Learning Plan. What skills do you need to learn? What is your plan to learn them? Who do you need to coach or mentor in the new conditions? Make a plan, set a schedule, build in accountability, and start taking action!

If you are adapting to changes right now in your organization, then complete the exercises now to **WIN at Change** before continuing to read.

WIN at Change

Written Inventory:

Individual Responsibility:

New Learning Plan:

For answers, we can turn to some great research. Harvard researchers learned "unambiguously that positive inner work life promotes good performance . . . people do better work when they are happy, they have positive views of their organization and its people, and are motivated primarily by the work itself. Conversely, with a negative inner work life, people are more likely to get distracted from their work, disengage from their team's projects, and give up on trying to achieve the goals set before them."[4] So, now you realize it not only "feels better" to have a positive attitude, but it gets results too!

It's much easier to be resilient in the face of stress and negative circumstances if you interpret them as temporary, local, and changeable (in other words, "It's going away quickly; it's affecting only one situation and not everything in my life; I can do something about it.") This point of view will immunize you against feeling helpless and depressed.[5] Even if the changes are permanent, you will have more control if you see them as an unfolding process where the present confusion and chaos will eventually yield new opportunities.

People who adjust well to change may be described as realistic optimists.[6] Here are a few ways to achieve realistic optimism.

- *Re-use strategies that have helped you handle changes in the past.* Remind yourself of a time when you were apprehensive at the beginning, but adjusted, and, maybe even benefited from those changes. Identify which of your qualities you displayed, or what thoughts or coping actions were helpful.

- *Adopt a growth mindset.* Dr. Carol Dweck[7] explains that people hold either a "fixed mindset" (where "what you know is what you know" and anything you don't know is perceived as a flaw) or a "growth mindset" (in which you see learning as a process, and you are willing to make mistakes for the sake of learning.) A fixed mindset keeps you on the Survival Under Stress cycle because you perceive that if change happens, you (and your current skills) will be left behind. A growth mindset helps you open up to new learning and encourages you to think about what you can control.

- *Be proactive and create a positive experience for yourself (the 50% rule).* Renowned CEO coach Marshall Goldsmith found that when employees are asked a passive question, such as, "How engaged are you?," they are likely to give answers with lower scores. But when employees are asked active questions, such as, "Did you do your best to be engaged today?," they show higher levels of engagement.[8] Thus, when you consider yourself responsible for embracing a positive outlook on change, you will make greater effort and create a more positive experience for yourself.

- *Serve a greater goal.* The Centered Leadership Model for Women[9] reminds us that people do their best when their work is imbued with meaning. If you can view setbacks and challenges as obstacles to be overcome in the service of a bigger goal and if you can embrace the feeling that the work you're doing serves a larger purpose for your life, the experience can motivate you.

3. Healthy Detachment

In addition to setting an intention and turning obstacles into opportunities, a third way to have more control over your day is to shift your perspective to one of Healthy Detachment. This is the best perspective when you've chosen to stay in a perpetually difficult environment, one in which a lot of effort will be needed to produce even incremental progress. Some appropriate situations for healthy detachment include: When your organization is undergoing change and you need to tolerate current conditions temporarily; when you have a difficult boss, colleague or business partner, but aren't yet in a position to change roles; or when you can't influence a political conflict, but are subject to its outcomes.

With healthy detachment, you continue to be engaged and make your best contribution, but you don't allow the outcome of your efforts to determine your internal state. Choose only battles that are worth your time and energy. Draw a line: Which negative impacts will you accept and which will you not? Be sure to keep on the "healthy side" of that line.

Here's a great example of healthy detachment in action. My client Amita was a senior leader in a high-visibility government institution involved with responding to the financial system crisis. She wanted to be an influential voice in the intense financial negotiations, but she didn't want to burn out. The encapsulation of her Horizon Point is **"Passionate Yet Detached Reformer."**

Though she saw herself as having "truth" (the right policy recommendations) on her side, Amita frequently faced resistance in her organization. Every day, she brought home stories of meetings where colleagues were critical not constructive, and where politics trumped good policy. Worn down by the constant frustration, she found herself being strident and unsteady.

Here's how Amita practiced healthy detachment: "I now take responsibility for what I can do in my 50%," she says. "But I am no longer emotionally attached to the outcome. I calmly and objectively present my point of view so that other people have the information they need to make a decision. I try to be respectful of people who frustrate me, knowing they may have perspectives or ideas that have worthy aspects to them, or that they may be privy to information that I don't have, or that they are not as informed as I am on the matter and need time to catch up. When others pick apart solutions I've offered, I am open to their input and ask them, 'how would you address this concern?' I appreciate that complex situations have imperfect solutions. I have learned to let go of getting to the outcome on the schedule I have in mind."

You too can minimize exhaustion and constant wear and tear by focusing on your 50%. In complex situations with multiple stakeholders, this means you drive a process but don't control the outcome. You accept that there's a natural order in which events will unfold and that it won't always go according to your desired timeline or route. When what you wished for doesn't happen, consider the whole context. If, for example, you weren't promoted, consider that maybe there's a better promotion opportunity down the pike (and actively seek feedback about how you should prepare for it). Or maybe that prospect hasn't made enough personal growth to be ready to benefit from your services (in which case, go find one who *is* ready!)

Few of us have the perspective or foresight to know why rapid global changes are occurring or even why a given organization is undergoing a major restructuring. From our limited perspective, we may only see the destruction of the current models but not the opportunities that may emerge. As long as you are empowered, as long as you are being who you need to be to get results in the present and future, you will be well positioned to thrive in your current environment and either lead or actively embrace changes in it.

ACTION PLAN

- Articulate who you want to be at your Horizon Point. Have fun coming up with your encapsulating phrase, image, or feeling. During the day, focus on fulfilling your Horizon Point person's qualities and attributes. That's how you stay in control of what you can control.
- Consider how you can turn obstacles into opportunities by turning the situation on its head and seeing how you can benefit. Begin by thinking of a current challenge, and try to look at it from the polar opposite perspective.

- If you are cultivating an attitude of Healthy Detachment, decide on your "lines in the sand." What is the line you won't cross? Once you know this boundary, you can be passionate and dedicated without allowing situations you deem as "too much" or "too far."

POINTS TO REMEMBER

- Setting an intention organizes your 60,000 daily thoughts and enables you to have more control over your day-to-day experience.
- Articulate the personal qualities that you want and need to be successful (your Horizon Point) and then act in the service of that ideal rather than just reacting to circumstances throughout the day.
- Turn obstacles into opportunities by changing your perspective and seeing the situation in its inverse.
- If you face workplace change, it can be helpful to prepare your plan to **WIN** at Change (make your **W**ritten Inventory, take **I**ndividual Responsibility, and formulate a **N**ew Learning Plan).
- Healthy detachment enables you to make your best contribution while protecting you from any negative impact of slow progress or resistance.

Recommended Resource

- To learn how to change your 60,000 thoughts a day from negative or worried to positive and focused, download a step-by-step audio training at www.sharonmelnick.com

4

Get the Calm and Focus
of a Yoga Class in 3 Minutes (or Less)
During Busy Work Days

"Set peace of mind as your highest goal and organize your entire
life around it."

—BRIAN TRACY, *motivational speaker and author*

Who is in charge of your response to stress? If you answered,
"I am," guess again. Until you begin to have more control, the thinking part of you—the "me" voice in your head—might not be as in
charge as you think. While you've been meeting deadlines, worrying
how you'll be judged, reacting to your colleague's interruptions, and
running out the door to commute home, your nervous system has
been creating automatic grooves of response patterns. In stressful
situations, we tend to fall into those well-worn patterns. And the conscious, thinking part of us is often the last to know!

Most of us are not taught the extent to which our experience is
influenced by our physiology—what goes on in the loop between the
brain and the body. Author Jill Bolte Taylor says we tend to pride
ourselves as "*thinking creatures that feel*, but biologically we are *feeling
creatures that think*."[1]

When we notice we are tired, wired, or angry, it seems to us as
though these states appear out of nowhere. We don't always know

how to change them. We sometimes turn to external substances for help—caffeine and sugar to boost our energy, food to comfort us, or alcohol or pills to wind us down for sleep—all because we don't know how to change our own physiological state!

We think stress comes from external demands, but what appears to be "out there" is actually being generated "in here." It's not the deadline itself that makes us feel stressed, but the perception of how much effort will be required to meet it (or what will happen if we don't), accompanied by the experience of being revved up inside.

The On Button and the Off Button

In your nervous system, you have a natural response to stress that includes an On Button and an Off Button. These reflect the two parts of your nervous system that are supposed to work in yin/yang balance. **Your On Button is your Sympathetic Nervous System (SNS). It energizes and focuses on problems.** It fuels you to zoom around all day. It reacts to external stimulation, such as an email alert, a refreshed Internet page, or the sound of your boss' voice. It switches on *automatically* whenever you have to muster energy.

Your Off Button is your Parasympathetic Nervous System (PNS). (In nonstressful moments, it regulates all of your basic body functions, including breathing, heart rate, and sleep cycles.) Once your stress system has been powered on by the SNS, your PNS tapers it off. The result: calm and rejuvenation. Your PNS helps you see the big picture, access your intuition, and improve your problem-solving skills. It enables so-called "shower moments" (sudden flashes of insight when you're away from work). It also helps you sort out the rational from the emotional, and thus prevents you from overreacting. You must activate your PNS *deliberately* in order to feel its effects.[2]

What if you could press that Off Button at will? You could recharge yourself throughout the day and have more reserve for when you come home. You could see trends as they emerge and use your intuition to come up with effective solutions for your future. You could be present at work and at home.

The key to Success Under Stress is being able to turn on and off at will. Now that's having control! That's what Stacy wanted: to know how to relax, to sleep through the night, and to have enough energy to be present with her children at home. And Dan wanted to have energy left over at the end of the day so he wouldn't just go home and "crash" at night.

Your Stress Response

It's important to appreciate that your nervous system was designed to deal with physical threats, but now almost all of our stress is mental. The most prominent of these mental threats can be identified by the acronym developed by David Rock: SCARF[3]—Threats (even perceived threats) to your **S**tatus (position and reputation), **C**ertainty (job or income security), **A**utonomy (ability to make decisions), **R**elatedness (connections to others), or **F**airness (being treated fairly). If you perceive that a situation will threaten one or more of these factors, the incoming information about that situation will be perceived as "dangerous"—as if a saber tooth tiger was running at you. As will be seen in Sections III and IV, that's why your confidence in yourself and the way you interpret other people's actions is relevant to your level of stress.

Remember, you have two parts to your nervous system that respond to demands for your energy and attention. Think of them as two teams of crewmembers on a ship. The first responder to any potential threat will always be your SNS crewmembers. They will provide a rush of adrenaline (which feels like an energy boost), followed by another stress hormone, cortisol, to initiate and persist in a response. They will light up your fear center and tell it to be on the lookout for other threats—and to err on the side of caution. They will send more oxygen to the lungs in case you need to do something physical (such as run away from a saber tooth tiger). You'll tune out everything else that's going on in your work and life, and you'll direct all your effort toward analyzing the situation: Is there is a danger? What can and can't you control? And what will it take to get out of the situation as soon as possible? In short, your SNS response is "React first, ask questions later." And it all happens within a few seconds.

Because of the constant stress from information overload and the demands of modern life, for many of us the SNS response has begun to spin out of control. According to a 2009 *New York Times* article,

> In most animals, a serious threat provokes an activation of the stimulatory, sympathetic, 'fight or flight' side of the stress response. But when the danger has passed, the calming para-sympathetic circuitry tamps everything back down to base-line flickering. In humans, though, the brain can think too much, extracting phantom threats from every staff meeting or high school dance, and over time the constant hyperacti-vation of the stress response can unbalance the entire feed-back loop. Reactions that are desirable in limited, targeted quantities become hazardous in promiscuous excess.[4]

Many of the signs of stress we recognize in ourselves—a racing mind, an inability to sleep, being on edge, snapping at others—reflect an overactive SNS. This is the Survival Under Stress cycle described earlier.

If your SNS hijacks your stress response, it prevents the counter-balancing PNS crewmembers from "tamping everything back down" to a state in which you're alert enough to work effectively, but not so revved up that you feel stressed. Your overwhelmed SNS will bias you toward perceptions of threat that perpetuate the stress response:

> *It's too much; I'll never be able to do it all; You're not good at presentations; You should feel guilty about your house not be-ing clean enough; Why was John promoted (or making more*

money than I am); I'm embarrassed that I'm so late to the meeting; It's going to be hard to figure this out by myself; What if I don't get another client?

When we have these thoughts, our SNS pumps out more adrenaline. We're angry. Fearful. In this hyperalert state, we can't think critically; we can't parse out the most and least valuable items on our "to do" list. Our memory for facts and details is compromised. So is our capacity to learn from past mistakes. We'll grasp at the first solution that comes to mind—and we'll get stuck.

When we perceive the situation negatively, it signals our brains to pump out more hormones that make us feel angry or fearful. And, that emotional state narrows the field of options to solve a problem. When dominated by the SNS response, we are unwittingly primed for more stressful events. Then we reactivate the cycle all over again (which we jokingly refer to as "same #%&, different day").

Before you learn to find your Off Button, remember that allowing yourself to be driven by your SNS will make it hard (if not impossible) to achieve your next success level. There are five reasons for that.

1. Your SNS seeks a quick fix—a squirt of dopamine, the neurotransmitter that lights up your pleasure centers when, for example, you cross something off your to-do list (even if it's not the most important item). It tees you up to take action that serves the short term, but won't necessarily pay dividends down the line. The main purpose of an SNS response is to eliminate whatever is currently stressing you out, with little regard for what may happen next. Holding on to an angry email overnight instead of sending it right away, or organizing your files, for instance, are not SNS-driven behaviors.

2. Your SNS works by comparison. It takes information about incoming situations and searches your memory to see how it links up with past experiences. It makes sense of new situations only as

they pertain to old ones. Your SNS is wired to see a situation for its potential threat: "Last time I didn't hear back from my boss or client right away it meant bad news. . . ." "Last time I had to present I felt embarrassed . . ." instead of searching for its future possibility: "My request to my boss was sufficiently complex that it may require thinking through before getting back to me. . . ." or "This presentation is my opportunity to show potential clients what I can do to help them."

3. Your SNS is self-referential—"Its all about me!"—because it evolved to help protect you from predators. "Were they blaming me? How can *I* protect my turf? How can *I* get what *I* need?"

4. When your system is in SNS mode, you have no protection against outside stresses. The moment someone says something that you take personally, that stimulus sets off a cascade of automatic responses. In contrast, when your SNS and PNS are coordinated, you have a brief period of time to think through a rational response.

5. Your SNS only knows how to turn on. The big secret is that it doesn't know how to turn itself off! This stress response system was developed for a short-term burst to protect us. It's useful when mobilized rapidly, then terminated. The problem for many of us is that we are always on.

When You Find the Off Button . . .

What happens in your nervous system when you know how to find the Off Button? Returning to our earlier ship metaphor, the SNS crew begins readying the forces just in case, but they don't take over the process. Instead, they summon the Captain of the ship. The Captain is your frontal cortex, the part of your brain responsible for thinking, reasoning, and decision-making. Your frontal cortex is what you think of when you think that "you" are in charge of your responses. You are the Captain!

In this scenario, your Captain steps in to lead the effort. She's a good leader and takes swift action. She immediately convenes the crewmembers from both the SNS and the PNS and commands that they work together to coordinate the emergency response. Notice how well they balance each other when it's done right: The SNS provides access to an intense ability to focus on a problem and plow your way through it. You're alert and ready to get to work. Meanwhile, the PNS counterbalances by seeing the big picture and tapping your intuition and creativity to solve problems. The PNS helps you learn new concepts and form new thoughts. It gives you the ability to take the emotion out of situations, see things from other people's point of view, and consider longer term consequences. This is the Success Under Stress cycle described in Chapter 1.

You can see the evolutionary advantage of being able to seesaw between zeroing in on a problem and taking a step back to look at the situation in its larger context.

This is why it's so important to follow the 50% rule and control what you can control. If your automatic functions—the SNS—take over and run the show (as they have for most people in our hyperstimulated world), you'll remain in a vicious cycle because your natural Off Button will be blocked. Science shows that while we don't have much trouble learning new ways, we do have trouble stopping old habits. We don't know how to let go. You must summon your Captain —the thinking part of you—to lead the process and to retrain and rebalance your system. Even the illusion of having control puts the thinking part of your brain in charge of the ship.

In sum, your SNS is your On Button and your PNS is your Off Button. You must actively do something to press your Off Button. The strategies in this book will help you access your Off Button, so you can bring your two systems into balance and, by extension, your life overall. That's why it's so important for you to control what you can control.

Balancing the On Button and Off Button

Be proactive about creating your on- and off-time. There are two ways to incorporate this idea into your everyday schedule. First is an overall approach to your day in which you have periods when you are "on" and periods when you are "off." Second is learning practices to help you press your Off Button and achieve a calm, expansive state.

Sprint-Recovery Pattern

Most of us work in a pattern that could be characterized as push-push-push all day long, ending in exhaustion each night. But a better way does exist: we can derive both energy and calm from the natural rhythm of our bodies.[5] Elite athletes who are trained for endurance rely on a sprint/recovery pattern—periods of intense effort followed by energy recovery and replenishment.

Be intentional about creating times when you are "on" and times when you are "off." During periods of recovery, choose between activities that are relaxing (deep breathing for example, or meditation) and activities that are energizing (such as exercise). It's optimal to alternate them.

Tony Schwartz, President and CEO of the Energy Project, is the foremost advocate of the sprint-recovery pattern. In the following excerpt from his blog[6] he describes two employees who work the same number of hours, but one accomplishes more and comes home with energy to spare for his family. It's a powerful demonstration of this pattern:

> Bill works essentially without stopping, juggling tasks at his desk and running between meetings all day long. He even eats lunch at his desk. Nick, by contrast, works intensely for approximately 90 minutes at a stretch, and then takes a 15-minute break before resuming work. At 12:15, he goes out for lunch for 45 minutes, or works out in a nearby gym. At 3 pm, he closes his eyes at his desk and takes a rest. Sometimes

it turns into a 15 or 20-minute nap. Finally, between 4:30 and 5, Nick takes a 15-minute walk outside.

Bill spends 10 hours on the job. He begins work at about 90 percent of his capacity, but by the end of the day he's averaging about 40 percent of his capacity. Over 10 hours he delivers 6 hours of work.

Nick puts in the same 10 hours. He starts at 90 percent of his capacity, and finishes the day at 70 percent. During his 10 hours, he delivered 6 ½ hours of work—a half hour more than Bill.

But because Nick is more focused and alert than Bill, he also makes fewer mistakes, and when he returns home at night, he has more energy left for his family.

The idea of a brief rest period in the workplace may seem foreign to you. It may make you feel guilty or fearful that you won't get all your work done, might miss out on a client opportunity, or be perceived as lazy. And, besides, you schedule is jam packed with meetings throughout the day, so how can you build in the sprint-recovery pattern?

If this idea is unheard of in your workplace, here are a few suggestions for implementing it. Stacy, for example, began her day with what she called "heads-down time." It began as soon as she arrived at the office (after a good protein breakfast) because that's a time of day when she has more control over her schedule. She used a technique you'll learn in Chapter 5 to eliminate interruptions in the morning and got in that first 60 to 90 minutes of work to start off the day with a solid accomplishment. That put her on the right cycle!

The quality of your recovery matters more than the quantity, according to Tony Schwartz.[7] Even if you only have three minutes in between meetings, spend it doing a recovery activity.

Next (and here's a perfect opportunity to Be Impeccable for your 50%), practice this sprint-recovery approach as you schedule your days on a go-forward basis. Be mindful of inserting recovery time at the slightest opportunity between your scheduled blocks (and don't allow back-to-back meetings all day). Begin blocking off 90-minute periods on your schedule and assign a specific deeper thinking task during that time. Then, allow for recovery time.

Compile a list of ideas of Off-Button activities you can do during your day. Build a repertoire of "recovery strategies" that span physical, mental, emotional, and spiritual approaches. Some examples from my Success Under Stress trainings are as follows.

Physical: Exercise, or even a few quick calisthenics, stretches, or easy yoga poses in your work area. Sit on a bench outside or even in your car to do breathing exercises (covered later in this chapter, as well as in Chapters 7 and 10). If there's a park or a body of water nearby, go for a walk or just sit down there. Walk to lunch. Put on headphones and listen to music. Meditate. Draw or sketch. Try aromatherapy (inhaling essential oils from a bottle or apply a small dot under your nose). Different scents have different purposes. For example, lavender, cinnamon, and vanilla are favorites for relaxation; grapefruit, lime, or eucalyptus will boost your energy. If you work at home, do chores, run errands, or cook.

Mental: Visualize your goals. Watch funny videos or judiciously circulate funny stories you read online.

Emotional: Schedule a time to talk with a friend or family member who lifts your spirits (you can also use the emotion clearing exercises you will learn in Chapter 10).

Spiritual: Appreciate the people who contribute to your life. Be grateful for all of the material things and opportunities you have. Remind yourself of your sense of purpose and the reason why you come to work.

A brief word about exercise and yoga. They are on my list of "greatest hits" to manage your response to stress. Regular exercise—

including a vigorous portion of each workout—is a must for Success Under Stress. It increases the number of transmitters in your brain responsible for helping you feel good and stay calm; it will prevent the aging effect that stress can have on you; it will help you learn and remember information; it can even prevent depression. Yoga is an ancient discipline that includes thousands of physical and mental exercises designed to strengthen and balance the body, rejuvenate the nervous system, and concentrate the mind. There are many different forms of yoga. Although yoga exercises are not explicitly included in this section, I have personally found great benefit in this popular practice. Anyone who regularly practices yoga is not only stronger and fitter but has increased energy and mental clarity. I strongly encourage you to find a type of yoga that gives you the benefits you seek. You can attend a regular class or take just a few minutes a day to practice key poses in your home. Exercise and yoga require a time commitment, and they take you away from your work environment. So they require planning. In contrast, many of the other strategies offered throughout this book can be practiced spontaneously at your office or in transit between destinations.

If you work out of your home or you're a salesperson who's on the road a lot, you'll need to be explicit about demarcating your "on" and "off" times. If you work at home, it can be easy to blend the two. Set aside a place in your home that's designated as a "work area." Decide on your plan: either you are always "on" in that space or, if you have the discipline initially, you can say explicitly, "I'm now off for the next 15 minutes." If you're on the road and "live out of your car," then either take your recovery time outside your car or mark time to listen to music or audio books, and then schedule "on" time to think about your next appointment.

Generally speaking, there are some gender differences on this particular point: Men seem to have an easier time taking breaks. In fact, men are 25% more likely to take a break and 35% more likely to do something just to relax than are women.[8] Women feel they have too much to do and too many people depending on them. This is accurate and understandable. When behavioral scientists first began researching stress, the standard way of thinking about the human response was the "fight-or-flight" pattern. More recently, however, a research team led by UCLA psychologist Shelley Taylor identified a different pattern of stress response that's typical for women—a pattern they summarized as "tend and befriend." In short, "females respond to stressful situations by protecting themselves and their young through nurturing behaviors—the "tend" part of the model—and forming alliances with a larger social group, particularly among women —the "befriend" part of the model."[9] Current research on women's leadership supports the notion that women are stereotyped as "taking care" and men as "taking charge."[10] Second, according to Carol Evans, CEO of Working Mother Media, "It's accepted in our culture that men should and are doing more tasks at home, but there is a lot less responsibility shouldering than there is task shouldering." In other words, women are getting more help on tasks, but as Evans sees from the responses of thousands of their readers, "It's the sense of responsibility that creates stress (picture a woman creating the list of chores for the man to do)."[11]

In short, women under stress are likely to take care of others and be the glue that keeps organizations and families together. But don't let that natural strength keep you from practicing the basics that will keep you healthy, energized, and effective. Review the sprint-recovery pattern data[12] and heed this advice: Finding your Off Button is neither an indulgence nor a low priority. It will make you a better performer, a better earner, and a better parent.

A tide of companies is embracing this concept. Many workplaces are beginning to get attuned to the need for uninterrupted times to accomplish work—as well as for times to recover. Savvy workplaces, such as Google, General Mills, and Genentech, are even establishing energy pods[13] and meditation/quiet rooms[14] Many have on-site gyms and/or wellness programs that are yielding hard returns.[15]

Raise the idea of a basic application of the sprint-recovery approach for your team. In my experience in leading team-effectiveness training, such teams are able to establish policies, such as "meeting-free times" or 45-minute meetings. You can start by introducing the concept to a team member who you think would be receptive.

If you're the boss, be a role model. Introduce this concept to your employees. One of my clients, Lucie, runs a financial firm with seven employees. Every hour on the hour the alarm goes off and one person leads everyone else in three minutes of vigorous exercise. The people who work at Lucie's company keep their brains and bodies fit and fabulous. Three minutes of hip-hop can get me going. How about you?

You also want to think about an extended Off Button for vacations or lengthier "getaways" from daily stress. Make sure you're not allowing your position or business to become so unwieldy that you never allow yourself the time you crave to get away and unwind. Try to spend time in natural settings, such as the mountains or the ocean; they help to reset your physical and mental rhythms.

This sprint-recovery strategy is on my "greatest hits" list of recommendations for Success Under Stress. Notice that it gives you control over the depletion and renewal of your energy resources—thus putting you on the positive cycle.

Now it's time for you to make your plan to incorporate the sprint-recovery pattern into your day. Take out your calendar, and think about how you can introduce that pattern at least once a day for the next two to three weeks. After that time, you can begin to schedule your days according to this pattern. Also, make a list of your preferred "recovery" activities.

Your Toolbox for Pressing the Off Button During Busy Days

The following strategies will help you find your Off Button. Again, your On Button is activated automatically throughout the day. Each time you push the Off Button, you will bring balance to your whole system, put your "Captain" back in charge of your ship, and gain access to the creativity you need to thrive in these times. Your Off Button helps you disengage from the automatic push of the workday and consciously find a way to renew by accessing your PNS.

There are numerous ways to press the Off Button. Exercises, such as breathing and meditation, have become popular because they can be done in your work area with no logistical obstacles, such as the need for props. **Many people find that the pace of their mind follows the pace of their breath**. According to neuroscientist Sonia Sequeira, PhD, when you slow your breath, or when you consciously regulate your breath in any way, you break automatic patterns of breathing and the unconscious emotional patterns that underpin them.[16] A breathing technique that focuses attention keeps you "in the moment" and helps center you so you'll make good decisions.

The benefits of "mindful attention" are now well established. Just to name a few, they include increasing brain size[17]; reducing activity in the part of the brain associated with the stress response (even for novice meditators)[18]; and lowering symptoms of burnout.[19] They have been found to improve concentration,[20] as well as the ability to "take the emotion out" of decision making.[21]

Numerous other research findings provide a relevant scientific basis for the benefits of breathing and meditative states. According to the data, they can improve our capacity for work.[22] If you're new to this, it might take a little practice, but you'll begin to experience some benefits immediately. Even when I demonstrate these techniques in my training seminars, participants begin to feel the calming effects within 90 seconds to three minutes. Readers who practice yoga, breathing, or meditation will enter recovery states very quickly.

Tools #1, 2, and 6 in the toolbox given below (as well as many tools in subsequent chapters) come from Naam Yoga, a practice recognized by the Yoga Alliance. According to its founder, Joseph Michael Levry, PhD:

Naam Yoga has a stress reducing, calming, and balancing effect that makes it a perfect remedy for the mind of a business professional. It has a neurochemical effect on the body so it rebuilds health and reverses the damage done over the years from chronic stress. It give you excellence based on your capacity to stop impulsive behavior and break the barrier of limitations, so that you may turn challenges into opportunities.[23]

TOOL #1: *The Mental Reset: Balance Your SNS and PNS*

If you've ever wanted a magic wand that could help you think clearly and focus when your head feels like it's going to explode, "three-part breath" is the technique for you! It can be used to relax after an intense period of concentration, to clear your head after a politically charged meeting, or as a mental reset in a moment when thoughts are crashing inside your head. By balancing and coordinating the two parts of your nervous system, it gives you access to two parts of your brain: the part that focuses on the problem and the part that sees the big picture with intuition. Each part of the breath also regulates and strengthens a different part of your body, making this exercise a general tonic to help you to triumph under stress. When done regularly, three-part breath will confer a long-lasting effect on your nervous system. You'll be steadier and less reactive in the face of stress.

Do three-part breath at least once a day for basic calming of your SNS (two or three times is even better). I know you're busy and it's hard to make time for meditation and exercise. But is it actually true that you can't carve out three minutes a day to keep your wits about you? The first few times you do it, notice if you're impatient to get the three minutes over with. If so, it means you're being ruled by your SNS, and you really need this technique!

Whenever possible, practice this technique with your hands in the position pictured in the photograph. Bringing your 10 fingertips together helps to balance the left and right hemispheres.

TOOL #1   The Mental Reset
Three-Part Breath

Breath: Inhale through the nose, hold, exhale through the nose all to the same count (example: inhale 5 counts, hold 5, exhale 5)

Hand Position: Bring together 10 fingertips to balance left and right hemispheres.

Duration: 3 minutes, 1–2x/day, or when overwhelmed.

For enhanced results, do it for one longer period (7–11 minutes)/day.

Learn more about the benefits of this breath and download an audio in which I count it out for you at www .sharonmelnick.com

Though you'll notice the effects from doing this technique just three minutes a day, you'll see a greater effect more quickly if you do it for a longer period such as 7 to 11 minutes daily. Because our schedules are packed, build-in a way to remember to do this mental reset during your day or establish a regular time for it.

I have taught the "three-part breath" technique to thousands of businesspeople, and they frequently tell me what a practical tool it is. One entrepreneur said, "You get the same calm and focus of a 90-minute yoga class, yet you get it in three minutes or less while at your desk!" After practicing the technique for just 90 seconds in my training sessions, participants report calm, focused, and clear minds. Overachievers in my training sessions for high-potential leaders often ask whether you can multitask your three-part breath while jogging or driving a car. The answer is No! Practice your three-part breath as a break and a reset from all other exertion (aside from the fact that you want to stay alert behind the wheel!)

I encourage you to incorporate three-part breath into your day. Scratch that. I *insist* that you make it a *must* in your daily routine! Before you go on to the next section, decide when you're going to do your three-part breath today and tomorrow—and for the rest of the week.

TOOL #2: *The Get-Back-to-Sleep Breath: Sleep Well and Wake Up Rested*

Sleeping is an integral part of finding your Off Button. During sleep, your body restores and repairs all its major systems so you can stay healthy, maintain an even mood, and concentrate during the day.[24] Enough sleep even lowers your level of hunger.[25] We all know from personal experience how cranky we are without enough sleep. It's also been proven that sleep-deprived people are more likely to dwell on negative events from the past.[26] (Now you may understand a little more about your boss or colleagues.) Yet, sleep is often the first thing to be traded off for an extra hour of productivity.

Some of you can't sleep restfully through the night. That's because your SNS is too revved up. According to Integrative Physician Sara Gottfried, "I see this pattern commonly in women who are super excited about their work, they turn on their laptop to work on the article or send off that last email, their brain gets overstimulated." They can't wind down and fall asleep because melatonin is blocked by blue light, and it backfires.[27]

With this in mind, create a Wind-Down routine before sleeping so that the transition between "on" and "off" isn't so abrupt. Begin 15 to 30 minutes before you actually want to go to sleep. Here are some of the strategies to include as part of your Wind-Down routine. When possible, introduce natural light, such as a candle, particularly one with a calming scent. Make a list of all of tomorrow's activities that are buzzing around your head today. Put yourself in a positive frame of mind by focusing for one to three minutes on what went well dur-

---

TOOL #2: The Get-Back-to-Sleep Breath
Left Nostril Breathing

Breath: Cover your right nostril with your right thumb or forefinger
and breathe exclusively through the left nostril. If you are using this
breath in the middle of the night, you can also try lying on your pillow
on your right side, so that your right nostril is covered.

Duration: 3–5 minutes to achieve calm so you can go back to sleep.

Use: To relax in order to sleep or to get back to sleep quickly when
awakened at night.

---

ing the day and what you are grateful for. Do an activity that helps
you relax, such as reading, sketching, or meditating.

There are also some natural ways to sooth yourself to help you
wind down. For example, chamomile tea is calming and soothing.
When you're stressed out, and especially if you live in a city, you regularly deplete the magnesium levels in your body. Taking a magnesium
supplement is a helpful addition to your "wind-down" toolkit.

Does your mind race before you go to sleep? Do you wake up in
the middle of the night thinking about work, and have a hard time
getting back to sleep? **Here is your magic bullet technique to help
you sleep well through the night so you can wake up rested.**

This breathing approach calms you down because it activates
your PNS.[28] When you use left nostril breathing, you'll be back to
enjoying those zzzz's within three to five minutes. Can you use it during the day? Sure, it will help to relax you, but it looks kind of funny.
Find a place you can do it in private or find a creative way of feel
comfortable covering your nostril in front of other people at work—
maybe get everyone else clued in to the technique as well!

TOOL #3: *Rapid-Clearing Breath*

Have only 1 minute? Spend it doing a rapid-clearing breath to rid
your blood stream of the harmful stress hormone cortisol.[29]

- Breathe in slowly to the count of 3.
- Breathe out slowly to the count of 6.

TOOL #4: *"Instant Bliss"*

I do the Instant Bliss exercise regularly when I'm sitting at my desk, waiting a minute for an elevator, or in line at a store. I start by intentionally relaxing the area around my eyes, then letting my shoulders relax and descend. Immediately and naturally, my body takes over and I allow a deep breath. There is a downward cascade in which my whole body "falls" and seems to relax. Once I've instantly entered that state, I try to keep doing long and slow and deep breaths to relax me and prolong the bliss for 1 to 3 minutes. Then, I'll take an energizing in-breath. Recharged, I'm ready to brave the world again! (I notice that within a few minutes of creating this instant oasis, I have what we refer to as "shower moments." I make my best connections between information I've heard that day and projects I'm working on.)

TOOL #5: *Meditation*

Meditation is a catch-all phrase that refers to a self-induced state of consciousness by bringing your attention inward. It has gained in popularity and, now, the importance, benefits, and acceptance of this ancient practice are mainstream, as evidenced by the numerous blue chip companies that are incorporating it and related activities into their talent development programs.[30]

There are different kinds of meditation. One popular type, Mindfulness Meditation, brings focused attention and increases the functioning in your front brain, which is responsible for thinking and decision making. As one expert says:

> Mindfulness is a focus on the current moment without the stress and anxiety of judging it. But as many employees know, work is all about the future and constant evaluation—the next item on the to do list, the misinterpreted email, or the

endless losing battle to accomplish more with less. A relentless focus on productivity has resulted in corporate environments that are more about mindlessness than mindfulness."[31]

Loving Kindness Meditation cultivates an internal state of compassion for others and increases the areas of the brain responsible for regulating emotions.[32]

A third type of meditation, the well-documented Transcendental Meditation (TM), uses an effortless repetition of a "mantra" (a sound, syllable, or phrase) to help you experience an expanded state of consciousness. According to the research, TM improves coherence of brain waves, which has been correlated with high levels of intelligence and competence.

Norman Rosenthal, psychiatrist and author of *Transcendence,* describes its personal effects: "Meditation helps because it gives us a break from the breakneck pace of the world. It lets the mind . . . slow . . . down so we can thinking more calmly and clearly. Since I started meditating I have noticed that many things that once seemed so urgent now seem less so."[33] Oprah Winfrey, a relatively new TM practitioner, joins other long-time TM meditators, such as Jerry Seinfeld, Russell Simmons, and many CEOs. She describes the effect on her company when many people there opted to learn and use the approach: "Only from that space can you create your best work and your best life. The people in my company who have been doing it report better sleep. Improved relationships with spouses, children, co-workers. Greater productivity and creativity all around."[34]

I know that when I meditate, particularly with the TM technique, it's truly a minivacation, and gives me the peace of mind we all crave.

To learn more how to get started, visit TM.org or contact a local meditation center near you. Many yoga studios and health clubs offer meditation classes as well. Find an approach that works for you and build it into your day!

TOOL #6: *Rejuvenate Tired Eyes*

Many of us sit in front of computers or other electronic devices for hours a day. Try these exercises to give some love to your eyes, which work hard for you!

Keep your eyes closed throughout the exercise. Rub your hands together briskly until they're warmed up. Immediately place the base of your palms in front of your eyes, about an inch away from them. Feel the heat penetrating and warming your eyes. Hold your hands there until the heat subsides and repeat as many times desired. Or, remain in this position for one to three minutes. Another method is to bring your thumb and the fingertips of your second and third fingers together and place them about an inch in front of your eyes. Point toward your eyes, as if you are sending a laser beam of healing energy their way (which is what you are doing!)

Now you're equipped with a handful of techniques you can use to find your Off Button. Some of them take only three minutes or less (meditation duration will vary depending on the kind you learn to practice), so you have no excuses! You've been looking for your Off Button, and now you have tools to incorporate it into your life. Start with the practice that resonated with you the most. Schedule it into your calendar, and make it a routine. What can you do to remind yourself to use the technique regularly whenever you need a brief "recovery" activity? Commit to doing it everyday.

My plan to press the Off Button during busy days:

_____

_____

_____

_____

ACTION PLAN

- Plan your day according to the sprint-recovery pattern and develop a repertoire of activities that help you press the Off Button.
- Designate a daily time to practice your three-part breath technique or establish a way to remember to use it "as needed" for a mental reset.
- Commit to learning about other practices you can do on a regular basis in order have regularly scheduled "off" periods.
- Review the other exercises in the Toolbox and use them on an as-needed basis to find the Off Button throughout your busy day.

POINTS TO REMEMBER

- Your nervous system has two parts: (1) an energizing sympathetic nervous system (SNS) and (2) a calming and rejuvenating parasympathetic nervous system (PNS). Your SNS gives you energy to accomplish tasks and tackle problems. It's wired to keep you focused on the past and solving problems in the way you always have. Your PNS helps you relax, see the big picture, access your intuition, and return stress back to resting levels when you get revved up. It helps you think through the entire set of possible solutions to problems and expands your outlook to be more future thinking.
- By balancing and coordinating the two parts of your nervous system, you can access both the focus-in-on-the-problem part of your brain and the see-the-big-picture-with-intuition part of your brain.
- As you begin to establish balance "on the inside," you will achieve more balance "on the outside."

Recommended Resources

- www.sharonmelnick.com. Download the audio in which I count out the three-part breath for you. You will also find numerous advanced exercises to find your Off Button during busy days.
- Tony Schwartz, *The Way We're Working Isn't Working*[35] www.theenergyproject.com
- David Rock, *Your Brain at Work.*[36] www.neuroleadership.org
- www.tm.org
- www.naamyoga.com
- www.heartmath.org
- Pick, M. *Are You Tired and Wired: Your Proven 30 Day Program for Overcoming Adrenal Fatigue and Feeling Fantastic Again.*[37]
- Gottfried, Sara. *The Hormone Cure: Reclaim Balance, Sleep, Sex Drive, and Vitality With the Gottfried Protocol.*[38]

5

Strategies to Reduce Overload
When Everything Is a Priority

"Time management is a misnomer, the real challenge is to manage
ourselves."
—STEPHEN COVEY, *Author,* The 7 Habits of Highly Successful
People

You will always have too much to do and not enough time. Every
day, we make thousands of microdecisions—where to give our attention, which task to initiate, how to respond to requests. As we discov-
ered, most of our reactions are automatic. For example, when emails,
instant messages, or calls come in, your SNS will automatically prepare
to divert attention to these communications. At such moments, you
may not have free will, but you do have "Free Won't."[1] When you hear
the beep or ringtone or are otherwise faced with an interruption, you
have a brief moment in which to make a choice: *Do I follow my wander-
ing eyes and open myself up to distraction, or not? Is the incoming stimulation as relevant to my priorities as what I'm doing now?* Don't just let
the barrage happen. Control your day before it controls you.

As discussed in Chapter 3, your brain is exposed to trillions of
stimuli every second, but it directs your attention only to a small, select portion of information. Meanwhile, it processes the rest, but at a
subconscious level. The key is to train your brain to attend to the in-

coming stimulation that is most relevant to your priorities and to filter out the rest. By keeping in mind the outcome you want, you can train your nervous system to pause and think through your next steps. The greater your clarity on your priorities, the more prepared you will be to tip the scales toward an intentional response versus an automatic one. (I encourage you to revisit the Ideal Day and Horizon Point exercises in Chapters 2 and 3 to remind yourself of some of the clarity you've already achieved.)

Think of each moment of your day as an investment of your time, energy, and attention. Like most investors, you want a "return on your investment" (ROI) in terms of progress and life balance. The aim of this chapter is to help you:

- Reduce the degree of overload by strategically clarifying the scope of your duties.
- Preserve your "bandwidth" for the most important matters.
- Use your time efficiently so you have more of it for what really counts.

These strategies are grouped into three sections:

–From "Everything Is Urgent" to "Prioritize Among Priorities"
–From "Always Available" to "Available on My Terms"
–From Effort to Efficiency

From "Everything Is Urgent" to "Prioritize Among Priorities"

"Don't tell me how hard you work. Tell me how much you get done."
—JAMES LING

It would be easy for me to say, "Just focus on your priorities." But we all know that managing your to-do list can be like herding cats! You have multiple competing priorities. Each pulls you in a different direction, and each seems urgent.

Figuring out your priorities is a process of clarification and communication. **Clarity is your best time-management tool**. When you feel overwhelmed, you can invariably trace it back to a lack of clarity somewhere in the chain of how priorities were decided. Clarity means knowing what your goals are and why they're your goals in the first place—and then aligning your day-to-day actions to help you progress toward those goals. The process also involves clearly communicating your choices.

Get started by answering the following questions. After each point of clarification, take up to three minutes to jot down your answers, so you can build a realistic, manageable daily schedule. Note that where relevant, separate sections are provided for readers who work in an organization and those who own their own business.

1. What is your role and what is your level within the organization?
Were you hired to produce a specific result or to set a vision and then manage the members of your team to actualize it?

For example, when I first started to coach Ed, he was a 45-year-old director overseeing datasets at a large government institution. In chronic crisis mode, his 12-hour days were spent putting out fires and chasing bugs in the system. He repeatedly had to tell higher ups that they would miss a deadline for implementing new processes. Talk about stress! A key reason for Ed's stress: he tried to solve the problems on his own instead of making plans for his direct reports to solve them and then holding them accountable. He began to do just that—and today he sees himself as the conductor of a symphony, not one musician playing all the instruments. He goes home an hour earlier each day and is being considered for a promotion.

Stress often results from operating above, below, or outside the level your job requires (except when you're working toward promotion and need to act at the next level to demonstrate you're already "acting the title"). You also create stress for yourself when you get "stuck in your job description" rather than keep up with the changing requirements of an evolving role. An HR director of a large hospital told me, "I watch managers do what they are comfortable with and not do their *real* job. It always leads to headaches." If you're unclear about your own level, take the time to discuss it with your manager and direct reports.

2. What are your and your organization's strategic priorities?

Clare Dolan, a vice president at Oracle Corporation, is excellent at setting strategic priorities. To identify your own priorities, Dolan suggests "Look closely at your organization's goals." Generally organizations set goals at the start of each year, and review progress against those goals quarterly. Part of your managers' work is to outline which groups or employees own specific aspects of the organization's goals. By carefully examining these goals, you'll be able to effectively discuss and agree upon your quarterly priorities with your manager. You might say, "I've reviewed our organizational goals for the year and believe that, for this quarter, my top priorities are . . . Do you agree with this?[2]

Once you and your manager are in agreement about your priorities for a particular quarter, Dolan recommends, "Link your daily 'To-Do List' with those priorities. You want to make headway on your priorities each day—don't allow yourself to fill your daily 'To-Do List' with things that aren't important."

I asked Dolan what to do if your manager doesn't clearly set and/ or communicate priorities across his or her team. "Be helpful," she said. For example you might say to your manager, "There appears to be some lack of clarity about our team's goals this year. Would you like me to gather a group of people to help clarify them?"

Here's a case of stress brought on by unclear objectives. Tim was a salesperson at a financial firm. His manager wanted him to mentor the less-skilled salespeople while continuing to meet his quota. His next level-up manager wanted him to contribute to the development of new products and business strategy. If he didn't fulfill his sales quota, he'd be penalized. And if he didn't deliver on the strategic requests he'd disappoint his manager's manager and lose an opportunity to expand his role. Stressed out, Tim was doing it all (and his wife wasn't happy either).

We proposed a schedule for Tim's time and then got approval from his manager and then his boss' boss: 80% on sales and 20% on new product development. We came up with a way for Tim to pivot in response to contingencies. For example, if he began to reach specific product-development milestones, it would be worthwhile to spend more time on product development; and if he didn't reach certain sales goals, he would need to spend more time selling.

He also sought clarification from his boss about her expectation that he spend time mentoring others. How much time, for example? And would he be recognized if his mentoring helped others land accounts? He used influencing skills you'll learn in Chapter 11 to get more administrative support to boost his sales effectiveness. Instead of attending every meeting on strategy development, he chose two of the five promising new product lines and spent time developing only those opportunities. These are just a few of the proactive efforts Tim made to set himself up for Success Under Stress. And yes, he was promoted on a fast track!

Just so you know you're not alone, I hear about unclear strategic priorities coming down from "the top" all the time. A lot of stress comes from our inability to control our priorities, which often leads us to try and do everything. Indeed, in the first quarter of 2012, the majority of executives said their biggest frustration is the organization "having too many conflicting priorities." Many companies "don't have a solid framework to decide which set of opportunities will lead to sustainable success."[3] Even companies can be on the Survival Under Stress cycle!

For a helpful perspective from someone who's been on the frontlines, I turned to Sheila McCaffrey, former director of strategic talent management at Pitney Bowes. "Stay true to your objectives," she advises. Then, she adds:

> Leaders will evaluate you based on the 'big things' and are
> less likely to take into account when you were in an assist role

on others' projects. Be strategic about the choices you make. Build in practices that will require you to take a pause before saying you will do an assignment. If you know you have an inclination to volunteer, then require yourself to think about it overnight, or have a set of questions about where you will think through how to accommodate that project into your schedule, and how you can uniquely provide value rather than allow yourself to instantly agree to take it on.[4]

Make sure you're seen as a team player, willing to take on tasks that are outside your defined role. But, as you do so, keep in mind the biggest deliverables you are responsible for, then offer to fill in on opportunities that are aligned with your goals, such as building a new skill or using a strength.

A final point to consider is the behaviors and tasks that your manager values. Track what your manager recognizes in team meetings and the "mantras" he frequently recites. Does your manager value speed? Deep thinking that leads to meaningful strategy? Accuracy, no matter how long it takes? Prioritize the activities that align with your boss's values.

Write down the clarifications you've just made. If you work in an organization, what are your and your organization's strategic priorities? What's most important to your manager? What's the one big project you must complete, even as you're making decisions about how to be a team player?

---

3. If You Are a Business Owner, What Are Your Strategic Priorities?
As a business owner, *you* should be determining the strategic priorities of your own business. You will dramatically reduce the stress of growing your business if you take the time to articulate a clear business model and a specific definition of success. Business owners often tell me, "I'm doing a million things. Help me feel less overwhelmed." I say, "Sure. I can help with that. Tell me about your business model." The response? Usually a blank look!

As business owners, here's how you can be impeccable for your 50%. Let's say you want to earn $100K this year. Can you help 10 people solve a problem so pressing that each would pay you $10K? Or, is your model to serve 100 people with a $1K service or product or 1,000 people with a $100 product? In the absence of a clear business strategy, you're doing the same "spray-and-pray" approach as Dan. You're attending networking meetings hoping people will see your value, accepting meetings with anyone willing to listen, trying every new marketing tactic you read about, and signing up any client even if you know they will aggravate you later.

Rich Schefren, founder of Strategic Profits, is a leading thinker on how entrepreneurs can "out think" their challenges. He describes overwhelmed and financially stressed entrepreneurs as "opportunity seekers" who go around collecting tactics and marketing strategies—what we often call "chasing after the shiny new object"—rather than "strategic entrepreneurs" who would instead ask, "What is the right tactic to help me get to my goals the fastest and with the least cost?"[5]

To shift from an "opportunity seeker" to a "strategic entrepreneur" you need to develop a competitive advantage that makes you the "go-to person" in your field. If you continue to compete in the "sea of sameness,"[6] *you'll stress over needing to work all the time in order to meet enough people to convert a few into customers.* Prospects may see you as a "nice-to-have," not a "must-pay-for." That's why it's key to tailor your marketing to the specific fears, frustrations, and desires of a clearly defined target—to the point where they think you know them inside and out. Then, they'll trust you to bring solutions to the table.

To grow your business, ask yourself, "Have you articulated what you do clearly enough so that other people could repeat it and refer to you?" If others are not referring to you, do you know if it's because they don't necessarily believe people need what you offer or because you haven't provided them with a compelling enough explanation of your unique value? (The resources at the end of the chapter will help you develop the answers to these fundamental questions.)

Here's how we worked out Dan's strategic priorities and business model.

- *Unique value.* Dan is a genius at financial modeling. He can review a financial plan and help clients save up to 30% more of their income. He also has a terrific "bedside manner"—using easy-to-understand metaphors to explain complex financial matters. So an important first step was to help him articulate the unique value he could offer clients. As we quantified the tangible and intangible benefits, Dan became more confident answering the question: "Why should a whale client come work with you?" He began using a new approach in initial meetings, one in which he educates prospects about their missed opportunities (rather than trying to "sell" them) and discusses how his system can make them more money. This approach "converted" more prospects into clients so he didn't have to fear he was missing out if he wasn't drowning in endless appointments.
- *Target client.* He narrowed his definition of an "ideal client" to a wealthy client with a specific risk profile, limited his networking and scheduling of first appointments to that subset of people, and became more willing to refer less valuable clients to his new associate.

- *ROI of time.* We dedicated his time to seeing new prospects (his strength) and involved his assistant in the administrative and operational processes that were bogging down Dan's schedule. We identified and concentrated on the business development approaches with the greatest ROI of time. By freeing up time to develop more business, Dan generated enough revenue to hire another person to take on follow-up work. This further freed him up to develop business and service his clients. You can see that Dan began to experience a positive cycle. As you'll learn in Section III, once he had a strong foundation in place, all he needed was the confidence to ask for the appointments with the whale clients.

What is your business model?

_____

_____

_____

4. What are your personal strengths?

Identify the top accomplishments in your life—the ones that you are truly proud of. More than likely, two to three core strengths helped you achieve these accomplishments. These strengths are your success factors. As Ralph Waldo Emerson wrote, "Nature arms each man with some faculty which enables him to do easily some feat impossible to any other." Sculpt your work role around your unique "faculty."

Often, business owners try to be "all things to all people" instead of concentrating on the strength that comes the most easily to them (and compels other people to purchase from them). "Any time you don't spend there sets you up for failure," says Rich Schefren. "Knowing your strengths can also help you work around obstacles in your business.... I see my flaws as my flaws and sculpt the business around me. For example, I hired a writer, so if writing sits on my desk for more than three days she does it or finishes it for me so I don't inhibit our productivity."⁷ Hire or trade with someone who has complementary strengths.

What are your unique strengths?

_____

_____

_____

5. What is your sense of purpose at this point in your career and life?
Use your Horizon Point to help identify your sense of purpose. This is key to being more intentional in your decisions. Choose the work activities that will help fulfill your Horizon Point. Further, although you likely "want it all," require yourself to consider what is *most important* in this next chapter of your life. Is it maximizing time spent with your family? If so, concentrate on efficiency. Is it developing as a leader who will advance in the organization? If so, choose assignments accordingly, and focus on opportunities to mentor your team. Is it generating more cash flow or having a passive income stream so you don't have to trade time for money? Is it building skills to make a next career move or developing an exit strategy for later payoff? Whatever it is, keep your sense of purpose top of mind and prioritize your schedule in the service of this outcome.

What is your sense of purpose in this chapter of your life and career?

_____

_____

_____

Tasks and Projects: Higher Value Versus Lower Value
Now you're going to bring together all the clarifications you just made and shift from being buried to investing your efforts on the work that will "move the needle forward."

Begin by dividing your to-do list into a two-column chart of "Higher Value" work and "Lower Value" work (see Figure 5.1). Higher value work is at the level of your role in the company and in direct alignment with your strategic priorities or business model. This work requires your unique strengths, and it serves your next-chapter purpose. Higher value work generally feels satisfying and leads to progress, not frustration and stress. Be aware that you may have trained your stress system to give you that familiar "dopamine squirt" (a momentary feeling of pleasure that comes from circulation of the neurotransmitter dopamine that activates your brain's reward centers) from ticking items off your list. Try to discern if items on your list are truly Higher Value, or just easy and convenient.

Start with an exhaustive list of everything on your plate, including outside-of-work commitments. Let a long list flow from your brain first; then categorize them.

After doing this exercise, Stacy (whose Horizon Point was "Top of the Mountain") became proactive about providing strategic advice

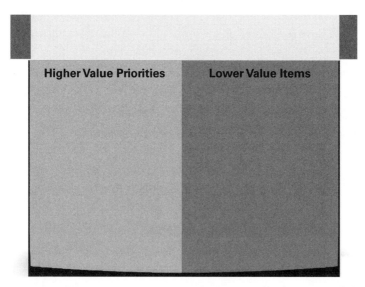

Figure 5.1 Use your answers to prior questions to divide your to-do list.

without getting bogged down in the contracts' technical aspects. No longer operating from the assumption that she had to fix everything, Stacy now saw the value of explaining to business colleagues how they could fix their own problems. She began to "own her value" as a manager, acknowledging the contribution she could make from "conducting the symphony" and advocating for her team, rather than doing all the work herself. She set clearer goals for her direct reports, mentored them to think like she does, and held them accountable for their goals rather than doing their work for them. She no longer tolerated an underperforming direct report whose work required her scrutiny. She sought out her manager to get clarity on her priorities. And now she filters each assignment: Higher Value versus Lower Value. Stacy reflected: "I've been giving a lot more thought to each action, and I'm in a much better place. I've gotten the workload under control." These days, she goes home at a reasonable hour and can be with her family. "I've done enough to go home, and I'm moving the rock forward every day. I go home feeling satisfied." As she began to view the workflow from her "Top of the Mountain" vantage point, she envisioned and proposed a team-wide reorganization to her boss. (He accepted her proposal and appointed her to lead the three sub-teams.)

What kind of dramatic reductions in stress and increases in productivity can you achieve with this exercise?

If you still have competing priorities, use effective time blocking —the allocation of specific times to work on a specific project or responsibility. There's more than one way to do this. Adopt an approach that aligns with your work style or situation. High-performing people tend to identify their most important project and will do whatever it takes, for however long it takes, to get it done. Rich Schefren points out the fastest way to achieve any result when you have multiple projects on your plate: If you have three projects ("A," "B" and "C") that will each take three weeks to complete, instead of doing one-third of each project every week over nine weeks, devote all of your attention to project A before going on to project B. You'll see a result in three weeks!

If you own multiple functions or are a solo practitioner, you can segment your day (or week) into time periods devoted exclusively to one kind of activity. If you're a business owner, you could decide to dedicate Tuesday and Wednesday to seeing clients, and Thursday to following up on the outcomes from those meetings. Group all of your sales meetings in a specific geographic region into the same day.

If you serve multiple masters, figure out which decision maker has the most power when it comes to awarding your bonus or promoting you—and do that person's work first!

Constantly review your list and stay on course. Surround yourself with people who have similar commitment to Higher Value work. Lead a team-based discussion to determine the Higher Value and Lower Value distinctions, so you can eliminate projects. This should have an uplifting effect on everybody!

Take time now (or schedule a time) to create your Higher Value Priorities versus Lower Value Items. Use Figure 5.2 to schedule time

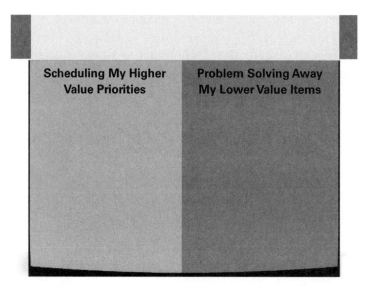

Scheduling My Higher
Value Priorities

Problem Solving Away
My Lower Value Items

Figure 5.2 Write down your plans to help you prioritize

for your Higher Value priorities over the next two to four weeks. Problem-solve away your Lower Value items.

> Q: But, what if I look at my "to do" list and become overwhelmed because everything needs to get done—urgently?
>
> A: In those moments your stress feels like it's rising inside of you. But you can stop yourself from getting on the survival cycle. Tell yourself that you will find a way to complete the important matters, then picture yourself in a state of satisfaction after the crisis is resolved. Next, get all the items out of your head by making two lists, one of substantive work matters (organized by project) and the other of quick, administrative items. Get started accomplishing the first of your "to-do" items right away, without dwelling on your long list. Put all of your attention on one task at a time and use the "5 Ms" to help you decide where to start:

- **Minutes**—How much time do you have right now to devote to your to-do list? If only a few minutes, then knock off *as many* of the quick items as you can. If you won't have time to complete an entire item soon, try to finish any remaining pieces of a substantive item first.
- **Metrics**—What is the bottom line metric that defines your success? If it's making money, do the single most important activity that will accelerate income. If your bottom line metric is delivering a project or result, consult your project management outline to determine which items are the next to be delivered or which you must problem solve to move toward completion of that phase of the project.
- **Mojo**—If appropriate, tackle the item that might not be the most urgent but will take the biggest weight off your shoulders and give you confidence and momentum to do other items.
- **Misfortune**—Which task, if not done, will cause significant risk or misfortune? Do that one!

- **Missing Communication**—If you have too many priorities because you've received conflicting requests or you've taken on an
  excessive workload, then make a plan to solve the problem at its
  cause (for example, lack of communication between two managers)
  before you proceed to perform tasks that only perpetuate it.

Q: How can I remember my priorities and not get lost in day to
day activities?

A: Many of my clients have success building in a simple 10 to 20
minute "Game Plan" in the morning (or at the beginning of the
week). They map out their "to-do" list, thereby adding structure to
their day. They also foresee (and incorporate into their schedules)
projects that are coming down the pike in a week or a month. Then,
they make daily updates. Each day, you triage crises and deal with
interruptions. As a result, you'll want to **plan your schedule ahead
of time as much as possible, so you are executing well thought-
out decisions rather than reacting in the moment.** Prioritizing
requires brainpower. It involves holding a lot of pieces of information
in your head and making decisions about them. Thus, you want to
"prioritize prioritizing."[8] Professionals who prepare a "game plan"
the night before (or the morning of) each day feel more organized
and productive.

Q: What if I feel I have to "do it all" and can't let go?

A: I get it! You don't have time to train someone else and, even if
you did, you believe that it won't turn out as well if someone else
does it.

You are well intentioned . . . but spread too thin. In this state, are
you attentive to the people and projects most important to you? Are
you keeping yourself on the survival cycle? If so, you're also depriving
the people around you of opportunities to learn.

Be on the lookout for opportunities to delegate assignments.
A lawyer at a pharmaceutical company offered wisdom on this topic

after years of pressuring herself to "do it all." She shares: "It's a juggling act. I've learned that you have to discern which balls are made of glass and which ones are made of rubber—you need to give the glass ones your attention and the rubber ones you can let bounce or pass to someone else."

If you can't delegate because you don't have people who can do the necessary work, be impeccable for your 50%. Take action to give underperformers every chance to rise to expectations (see Chapter 11 for a script). But, if they don't show progress, don't be shy about finding someone else who will. A lot of stress is the result of putting up with poor skills or avoiding direct conversations about someone's underperformance because you want to be "nice." Take responsibility for your part by treating the person with respect but do help them transition out of the role.

When you delegate, be intentional. Paint a picture of what success looks like and make sure your direct reports see the picture in their heads too. Don't say "Do x and y" and let them walk out the door. Have them actively describe their plan to accomplish the work. Establish expectations and a check-in plan at the outset. Do you want them to run with the project and not show it to you until it's finished? Do you want to establish milestones at which they'll check in with you to make sure they're on track? Establish the communication plan and schedule any check-in dates up front. They get to support you in bringing forth your brilliance, and you get to support them bringing forth theirs!

> Q: How can I say "No" without feeling guilty or hurting the feelings of others?
>
> A: Do a gut check. Is your sense of obligation coming from truly wanting to do the project or more from the discomfort that comes from saying "no" to another person who's expecting something from you? If you are prepared to say "no" to an assignment, make sure you have "air cover" from your manager. Here are guidelines for how to say "no" and feel okay about it.

- **Be Straightforward**—Give the person a clear and concise message that you can't do it or can't do it on the timeline they have requested. Ask for more time or another arrangement. Reset the expectation!

- **Be Sincere**—Explain the situation: "We've just had an adjustment in our group's priorities, and I'm now being deployed to. . . . This is going to impact my ability to contribute to your project." If necessary, appeal to a higher authority: "I'm working on a project for (shared authority figure) and have to focus on that for now." Share your genuine feelings: "I was excited when you first asked me about this because . . . and I gave it serious consideration," or "I'm genuinely sorry I can't help you out here. . . ." You can be gracious, and you can be apologetic if you sincerely feel that way. "I really appreciate you asking me, but I am fully committed now," or "I just don't have time and bandwidth to give you my best attention now. Let me recommend someone who may be able to help you." If it's particularly hard for you, you can even "blame" someone else: "I've promised my (husband, son, coach, etc.) I'd be home for dinner three nights a week" or "I'm committed to being at my daughter's soccer game on Saturday. . . ."

- **Be Social**—Say "no" to the specific request, but try to preserve the longer term relationship. Ask if you could make a less demanding contribution, such as putting together some talking points rather than attending a meeting. Offer to fulfill the request on another occasion, or when you have more time. Or, maybe you could refer someone else. Offer to do what you *can* do, even if it doesn't fulfill the original request. And, make sure you ask the person about the situation the next time you see him or her. This shows you still care about the outcome.

Remember the purpose you articulated for your life and consider the "no" in the context of preserving energy and building momentum toward that purpose. As Mahatma Gandhi said, "A 'no' uttered from the deepest conviction is better than a 'yes' merely uttered to please, or worse, to avoid trouble."

Q: How can I prevent my boss, partners, or clients from piling on the work?

A: You may be thinking that all of this advice would be helpful if you could only implement it! An ever-increasing stack of work usually signals an opportunity to communicate with those assigning it. Do what you can do in your 50%. Say "yes" as often as possible, but instead of just presenting your game face and saying "okay" to additional requests, think through the components of each assignment with regard to:

- The time it will take.
- The scope of the project.
- The resources required.

Try to say, "yes" to the request, and then negotiate the terms of the assignment. For example, "To get it done in the time requested, I'm going to need XYZ additional resources," or "To finish this using the resources we currently have, I may need to adjust the timeline." You can apply your experience and say, "Given the current resources and the tight turnaround time, we may need to start by getting only the first phase done by the end of the week, and then the second phase by mid next week." As circumstances change, you will need to revise your priority list. Go to your manager or client with recommendations on how to adjust priorities, and then ask for their input. Always remember to be impeccable for your 50% and bring a solution, not just the problem!

If a client is piling on work, inquire about the purpose of the request and the timeline to see if you can accommodate the request without addressing the full scope of what is being asked. For example, if your client calls on Friday afternoon at 4:30 for a requested proposal due Monday morning, avoid a knee-jerk reaction. Instead, you could ask about the purpose behind the request. The client may only need a basic cost estimate and some bullet points, rather than a full proposal. You could also offer to be on the conference call Monday morning to provide backup information. Negotiate the terms to get the work done in a way that keeps you "in the zone."

Q: Is there anything I can do about the amount of time I waste in meetings?

A: Yes. Raise a discussion with your group. I recently led a group training for a consumer products company in which the members decided that all meetings would be 45 minutes (to allow for "recovery time"), that meeting invites would list whose presence was expected and whose optional (so you could attend only mandatory meetings), and that meeting notes would be available for all who want to know the decisions but didn't need to attend.

Further, Monica Worline, PhD, cofounder of Vervago, a firm specializing in providing solutions for knowledge workers, says, "If people aren't being precise in their thinking and careful in their communications, they spend a lot of time talking about things that aren't necessarily the priority or the heart of the matter. They don't drive the project forward. You spend all that time in meetings then have little time left in your day to do thinking and to advance on the challenging problems."[9] Countless hours we've all wasted in that swirl! Additionally, if we aren't concise when answering questions in meetings with senior executives, we might not get the results we desire. Worline's company teaches a skill set called Precision Question and Answering, in which you use your critical thinking skills to surface relevant information (instead of having meeting participants randomly give their thoughts or provide justifications for why work wasn't done).

According to Worline, use a core answer such as "yes," "no," a number, or a date. Be impeccable for your 50%. Stay on course toward the meeting's specific intended outcome. And after you've answered the question, stop talking. If appropriate, take more control over meetings: send out agendas, offer to chair the meeting, bring up the concept of the 50% rule on your team, and brainstorm all the ways it can be applied—including in meetings.

Be on the lookout for "open loops" in your meetings. These are the many initiatives, thoughts, or projects without a clear timeline or next steps. The items that people are "talking about talking about" just take up mental RAM. List your open loops, and write down what you can do within your 50% to gain clarity going forward. How could you accelerate a decision? Could you suggest shelving an initiative and identifying the specific criteria under which it should be revisited? Can you make any unilateral decisions and cross some items off your list?

In Part I we went through a process of clarifying what's most important to you and then building your schedule around those priorities. We also problem solved some of the typical obstacles to focusing on your highest priority work. Like a superhero, swat away those lower priorities and get busy on the ones that will move your needle forward to help you enjoy your Ideal Day more often.

From "Always Available" to "Available on My Terms"

> "We are the most overinformed, underreflective population at any time in history."
> —ROBERT KEGAN, *Professor, Harvard University*

While interruptions are inevitable, view your time, energy, and attention as precious nonrenewable resources to be preserved. Most office workers are interrupted an average of seven times per hour— approximately 56 times each work day. Typically, these distractions add up to 2.1 hours a day.[10]

ACT in Response to Interruptions

You may think that since interruptions originate with other people, they should be the ones to stop. You hope that they'll read your mind when you resent them for distracting you! Based on what you've read, I hope you're beginning to see that you always have a choice. You can control your 50%. With any given interruption, you can use the acronym A-C-T to figure out one of three possible responses:

A: Allow (or accept)
C: Cut it off at the pass (or curtail)
T: Triage

Accept or allow: If you allow an interruption, give it your full attention. Take the phone call and stay on as long as it takes to resolve the issue. Read through the email and make a full response. You need thoughtful and strict criteria for determining which situations should warrant this response. Here are some examples:

- Your manager or clients expect real-time availability.
- There's a significant risk to service levels.
- A high visibility project can't move forward without your input.
- The interrupter is a mutually supportive friend who generally doesn't waste your time.
- A personal or family emergency.

From now on, you can choose to accept or allow interruptions if they meet your preset criteria. These are matters you have thought about and considered to be as important as anything on which you are currently working.

Cut it off at the pass (or curtail): Obvious ways to avoid interruption include turning email notifications off or not picking up the phone. You can also "schedule interruptions" so you'll have more control over when others contact you. For example:

- Schedule regular meetings with people who frequently need your input.
- Assemble a FAQ document with comprehensive answers to frequent questions—and include a reference to it on your voicemail or signature line of your email.
- Arrange "buffer times" in which to deal with unexpected matters or callbacks.
- Hold "office hours" and let people know the best times to contact or expect a call back from you to deal with urgent matters.
- Follow the example of Peggy Traub, CEO of Adesso, a manufacturer of contemporary lighting and home decor. When employees have issues to discuss with her, they join her on her weekly lunchtime "walk with the boss."[11]
- Find an empty conference room, quiet local café or, if appropriate, a spot in your home. Tell people you are taking uninterrupted time. Let them know you are available by cell phone for situations that are urgent. But be responsible for your 50% by defining what "urgent" means to you (you can be sure it will mean something different to them).
- If your direct reports or assistant are the source of interruptions, empower them to take greater ownership and teach them how you think about solving problems. Let them know you consider them capable of solving problems and that their performance will be evaluated based on how much they take ownership of situations. Encourage them to be solutions-oriented so you only need step in when it's truly necessary

Triage: Allow a brief interaction between you and the interrupter solely to determine how to deal with the interruption. Just like the nurse who greets you in the emergency room, your intention is to understand the patient's need and then swiftly figure out a response. With the ER nurse image in mind, pointedly (but pleasantly) ask a few questions that will give you clarity over the situation. The right questions can help you craft a mutually satisfying plan—or even help you determine that you don't need to get involved at all. Make a list of three to five questions that are relevant for your circumstances. Post them in your office, so you can easily refer to them in these situations.

One hospital manager who learned about A-C-T through my on-line productivity program, even said, "I saved at least an hour a day by not dropping what I was doing to get involved in others' stuff and then having to reset myself to come back to my own work. Now I'm not taking on problems that I don't own and, when I do have to get involved with others' problems, I can do so on my terms."[14] Notice how she is controlling what she can control! What will you do with an extra hour each day? ACT on interruptions to find out!

What were some key interruptions over the past week or so? Take a moment to reflect on how you would use ACT to handle them differently. Chart 5.1 shows a log that Stacy completed to handle interruptions. Complete Chart 5.2 to help prepare you for how to handle common interruptions.

Be More Intentional About When You Are and Are Not Available

Technology literally opens up the world to us. And, it sets us up to live with an ever-present temptation to be available. Aside from the occasions when your accessibility is required, how much you make yourself available is up to you, not the people around you.

It's *your* choice: Have you ever tried to pinpoint why you allow interruptions? Is it just a default—a nervous system untrained in the use of its Off Button? Or, is it a good intention gone out of control? "Our addiction to digital devices has more to do with an underlying need to feel wanted and important. ['We believe that] being a successful member of the middle class society is showing our dedication to professional work and being available at all hours of the day.' . . . And yet, this dedication does not translate into increased productivity. . . . People who are regularly bombarded with different types of electronic

WHO	WHAT	A-C-T APPROACH	PROBLEM SOLVE
John	Needed last minute recap of company protocols for his presentation to clients (does this often)	TRIAGE	Train John that I need at least 24 hours to prepare comments for his client meetings. Talk through what his definition of "urgent" is to identify what is truly urgent.
My Sister	Phone call to chat	ACCEPT	Schedule time to talk to her during a "recovery" break —not in the middle of my focus time
Boss	Multiple emails with work requests	ACCEPT / CURTAIL	Proactively give her status updates. Ask her to indicate prioritization of emails or bundle requests so I can better respond. Set up more regular one-on-one meetings if necessary
Elsie	Request to volunteer	CURTAIL	Send to private email and bundle for evening rapid response
Child's doctor	Appointment phone call	ACCEPT	Will take less than 2 minutes

Chart 5.1

WHO	WHAT	A-C-T APPROACH	PROBLEM SOLVE

Chart 5.2

information . . . do not pay attention as well as those who prefer to complete one task at a time."[12]

We tell ourselves, "If I don't talk to them, I will seem rude," or "I'll feel guilty," or, "If they need help, I have to help them." Is that being responsible for your 50%—or for someone else's? Or perhaps you think, "I'll be negatively evaluated if it's my boss and I don't pick up the phone," or, "Those prospects won't wait to hear back. They'll just take their business elsewhere." These are fear-based assumptions that may or may not reflect reality. So, let's look at the situation objectively.

Some bosses and clients want you to be responsive 24/7. They expect you to return their calls within a nanosecond. But many don't. Some expect you to reply to their weekend email. Others write when they have time, but they don't expect you to respond until Monday. *Ask* them about their expectations; then you'll know. And, to help you bring more intention to a plan going forward, take a moment to consider why you make yourself so available.

To control the inflow of connectivity, come up with preset criteria similar to those you developed to A-C-T on interruptions. Which aspects of your availability underpin your purpose and which don't?

For example, taking calls on your cell phone on your way home may help you wrap up key issues or keep in touch with dear friends, but does keeping the phone by your bed also fulfill that purpose? When you own your value as an employee or a service provider to your clients, people will understand and actually respect you for only being available when you can give them your full attention. Even those of us who are hard driving and career focused derive greater satisfaction from our jobs and lives when we experience built-in downtime.

If 24/7 connectivity overwhelms you, you're not alone. It's a universal problem. In fact, a number of progressive companies are addressing it by taking steps to ban emails on weekends or after hours.[13,14] If you're a leader in your organization, why not step up and put together a policy that's in everyone's best interest?

My new criteria for when I will and will not be available:

_____

_____

_____

Q: How can I turn off my connectivity during the day so I'll have time to think creatively?

A: Were you a better or worse version of yourself before you were bombarded with electronic messages? Research shows that the more you are addicted to email and electronic messages, the more you experience degradation in your thinking quality.[15] You want to build reflection time or what I call "connect-the-dots time" into your schedule on a regular basis.

The world's greatest innovations? They are definitely *not* initiated by people on the Survival Under Stress cycle! Innovation comes from people who take the time to "marinate their thoughts"—who seek out opinions, listen carefully to key stakeholder input, and reflect on what they see, hear, read, and experience. "Constant communications mean you regularly suffer cognitive overload, never focusing on any one thing for any meaningful amount of time," says Nicholas Carr, author of *The Shallows: What the Internet is Doing to Our Brains*. "There are certain types of creativity that come only from undivided attention, and by losing the ability to focus, you might be sacrificing one of the most important sources of long-term innovation."[16]

So, when you're feeling overstimulated, with thousands of thoughts running through your head, stop. It's a signal that your SNS is spinning out of control. You need time for counterbalance and reflection. Schedule your day to allow some time to process your thoughts, or schedule an hour or two a week of dedicated time. "Connect-the-dots time" is not a luxury. Protect it fiercely. You'll find that this reflection time will make you "smarter"—better able to come up with innovative ideas and be prepared in meetings.

I found that balancing stimulation and reflection was one of the most essential processes for completing this book. Every day I would take in the words of my clients, gain insight from experts, and read articles and books. When I felt the early warning signs of being overwhelmed, I would take a step away. I can assure you, my best ideas never came when I was engaged in my busy day, but rather when I stopped for a scheduled "connect-the-dots time" or when I went for a run, prepared dinner, or did my three-part breath (or other "Off-Button" activities discussed in Chapter 4). Even Albert Einstein hinted at this balance of stimulation and reflection. "You can't solve problems," he wrote, "with the same level of mind that created them."

What is your plan for how you will build in time to connect the dots?

_____

_____

_____

_____

Finally, try to expand this time into periods when you're fully "unplugged" from electronic devices. When you first allow yourself to relax or have solitude, the absence of noise may make you feel anxious. But once you settle in, you'll begin to experience peace of mind and a state of creativity to which you'll want to return again and again. Begin with an hour on the weekend, work toward the entire weekend and, eventually, a fully "unplugged vacation."

From Effort to Efficiency

"It's possible for a person to have an overwhelming number of things to do and still function productively with a clear head and a positive sense of relaxed control."[17]
—DAVID ALLEN, *Author, Getting Things Done: The Art of Stress Free Productivity*

So far in this chapter, you've learned some ways to clarify priorities, reduce interruptions, and free up time. We've covered the "what to do." In this section we'll review "how to do it." "Process Before Content" means you consider the most efficient and effective approach *before* diving in. Running from meeting to meeting and task to task under pressure to "get it done" isn't intentional. It may lead to inefficiencies or rework. There will always be too much work, so the question is: How can you get better quality work done faster?

Serial Monofocus Instead of Multitasking

When we're on the survival cycle, many of us think that multitasking will help us meet the demands. This is a myth! In reality, you lose efficiency and focus each time you have to switch between topics and projects. As you do that over the course of the day, you can take up to 30% longer to complete a task and make twice as many mistakes.[18] Who do you think performed cognitive tasks better in an experiment

—multitaskers or study subjects who were high on marijuana? You guessed it: the multitaskers did worse.

What's the best way to manage your attention? Serial monofocus. Our working memory can only hold up to seven pieces of information. When you multitask, you have to let go of some of what's in your working memory to make room for the new task; in this state, you can't rely on your memory.

One of the most important skills for success in the New Normal is the ability to give your full attention to what you're doing in the moment and then shift your full attention to the next task. When you arrive at what I call "the moment of crunch"—when everything seems to be coming at you at once, Professor Joel Nigg of Oregon Health & Science University advises, "Put 100% of your attention on the crisis and don't let your mind be split off. If you give time to an item, but don't solve it, then you have to come back to it. Instead, write down the thing that has to be done, be fully present to that person or that problem and give everything you've got to finish it. Then move on to devoting 100% attention to the next situation."[19] When you achieve this, according to David Rock, "You perceive more accurate information about these events. You also become less imprisoned by the past, your habits, expectations."[20] It will help you relax and make good decisions in that stressful moment.

Get It Right the First Time

How many times have you left a meeting thinking you had clear marching orders, but then didn't deliver what the person wanted? Urgghhh! Do what I call "scaffolding." Get the information you need from the delegator to fulfill the request before you leave the interaction. First, visualize the steps you will need to follow once you are back at your desk. Then, ask the questions you know you'll encounter as you carry out the assignment. Sometimes delegators are unclear in their own minds about the tasks they assign. For example: Do they want a high-level or detailed data analysis? Data by month or year?

Whom else should I copy on the report? Before you dive in, reiterate what you heard and how you plan to carry out the task. Then, ask for confirmation. This will also help you avoid delivering too much or not enough detail.

Does your manager or client change their minds all the time? Here's what you can do in your 50%. Help them think through the situation by playing out the scenarios in the moment. This will prevent thinking it through later and then changing their minds. Perhaps say, "We tried it this way last time and this is what happened. Should we try it another way this time to prevent that unintended consequence?"

Meeting Scheduling and Preparing

Do you schedule meetings according to whether there is a slot available in your calendar? I had a feeling that was the case! This approach lacks intentionality. The following suggestions apply irrespective of whether it's you or someone else doing the scheduling.

When a meeting is requested, take a minute to ask some key questions. For example: What is my contribution expected to be? Who else is attending, and who is facilitating? If the meeting is not closely tied to your objectives, consider declining the invitation or requesting a meeting summary. Clarify whether the meeting is devoted to multiple topics or just yours. If the former, perhaps inquire whether you could attend only for the portion that pertains to your work. Send someone in your place, or ask to call in instead of appearing in person. And, schedule time for your preparation and follow up at the same time you book the meeting. When running meetings, have a clear agenda, understand each person's objective, and end the meeting as soon as the outcome is reached.

Exercise Your Power in the Beginning

The power to get results and prevent problems resides at the *beginning* of a process, project, or relationship, not at the end. In fact, productivity research indicates that every minute spent planning saves nine minutes in botched execution. As the old saying goes, "A stitch in time saves nine."

Cindy Morgan, Vice President of Organizational Development and Learning at New York University Langone Medical Center, echoed this when explaining why she had been successful in initiating large-scale organizational change processes. "The power is at the beginning," she said. "The upfront contracting piece is vital. If the scope is too big or there aren't enough resources or time, you've created a stressful scenario because the effort could potentially fail. The initial phase is your time to consider, 'what is the minimum and the maximum we could do,' and then balance that with what your client needs."[21]

Whether you're a team leader or a team member, follow project management guidelines to get thorough agreement up front on the premise of the project, the plan to implement it, and the monitoring of progress.

When entering into a new relationship with a business partner, an assistant, or a manager, it's better to overcommunicate than undercommunicate. Ask about their preferred communication method, and give them the "User Manual" of how best to work with you. For providers of professional services, the initial client contracting phase sets the expectations for the overall relationship—and it's always harder to go back and amend than to get it right up front. At this point you feel vulnerable because you haven't yet received their business and proven your value. So, instead of laying out the terms and describing what's outside of your fee structure, you may think, "Let's just get them in the door and worry about all that later." If this is your approach, once they've engaged you, avoid setting up a stress cycle later by negotiating the terms of extra client time or revisions up front.

Pruning Time Wasters

What are the five biggest time wasters in your day? Do you know *why* you do them? For example, if you turn to surfing the Internet, understand why. Are you trying to manage your anxiety or boredom? Are you constantly checking email because you like to feel needed? Is it procrastination because the work you have to do is too complex? Do you lack a clear purpose for your surfing time? Are you "looking for love in all the wrong places," seeking meaningful connections via your social media interactions? If so, figure out a way to fill these underlying needs more constructively, or limit the time you spend on them.

Can any of your time wasters be automated or systematized? I've recently begun using a system that automatically filters and organizes emails based on rules I created, and it saves me literally a few hours each week. Score!

There may also be an opportunity here to be a leader in fostering an office culture that limits universal time wasters. Many organizations are instituting policies that support employees' time to think and complete work.[22]

Taming Email

People often complain that excessive email often drains their time and mental energy. For advice I turned again to Clare Dolan, a vice president at Oracle Corporation. She radically transformed email use in her organization and, in the process, helped her employees increase their mental clarity at work. Dolan explained, "Most people don't think at their best if they are receiving 100 emails a day. I asked the folks in my organization to remember that email is simply one method of communication—in other words, it's not 'the work'! My team responded to this by becoming more judicious with their email and, in turn, started challenging and supporting one another to contain their email volume. As we did this, we achieved more and found ourselves to be less stressed."[23]

No matter how your organization-wide efforts go, you can always take back control of your own email inbox. I recommend the work of David Allen (and have included his Website among the recommended resources at the end of this chapter). His approach will help you sort emails into those that require immediate action (in which case you would either take action, get it off your to-do list, and out of your inbox, or else make a plan to delegate or defer it) or don't require immediate action (in which case you would consider archiving or deleting it). Unless you are in a customer service kind of role that is premised on real-time email responsiveness, set up regular times to check it rather than having email as your default screen. (Instead get an inspiring desktop display/screen saver that recalls your Horizon Point!) Inform people about your email availability and when they can expect to hear back from you.

We've covered a number of ways to become more efficient and effective. You may want to consider trying one of these strategies for a week or so, until you get the hang of it, or picking out the ones that resonate with you (rather than trying to remember to implement them all at the same time.)

ACTION PLAN

- Go through the exercises in the clarification process using the Higher Value versus Lower Value work chart. This will create many opportunities for you to clear hours of work off your schedule and free you to concentrate on what matters most.
- Fill out your Interruptions Log and be prepared to minimize the time drain of future interruptions. Decide on your preset criteria to Allow, Curtail, or Triage Interruptions.
- Make a "go-forward" plan for how to be available on your own terms.
- Review the approaches that will help you make any work interaction more efficient and help you get a better result. You may want to rehearse them in your mind or write yourself notes where you'll see them in the heat of the moment (e.g., at the top of your notepad).

> *POINTS TO REMEMBER*
>
> There are three approaches to control your day before it controls you.
>
> * Go through the steps in the first part of the chapter to determine the unique strengths around which you want to build your position or business. Then determine the level of activities that you are especially suited to and required to carry out—and be fiercely proactive about problem solving away all the other matters you are spending time on.
> * To preserve your bandwidth, have more awareness about why you're always available for responding to communications and interruptions. Come up with preset criteria that will help you respond intentionally when requests and messages arrive. Build in time to "connect the dots" in addition to the work that keeps you busy throughout the day. Use the acronym A-C-T (Accept, Curtail, or Triage) to help you sort through how to respond to interruptions.
> * Before you dive into a task, spend a moment figuring out "how" to approach it so that you can complete it efficiently and get your desired result without rework.

Recommended Resources

* David Allen, *Getting Things Done: The Art of Stress-Free Productivity*[24] and programs at www.davidco.com
* Rich Schefren, *From Frustration to Freedom for Entrepreneurs* and www.strategicprofits.com

To find your strengths:
* Strengthsfinder 2.0 www.strengthsfinder.com/ or Kolbe Index http://www.kolbe.com/

For precision question and answering to think critically

• www.vervago.com

Technology tools

• Sane Box—email inbox filter. www.sanebox.com
• Rescue Time—shows how you spend your time on the Internet and how to minimize wasted time. www.rescuetime.com

Solutions for Self-Imposed Stress:
How to Care Less About What
Other People Think

The self-talk you hear all day long is like a "mental iPod." If you aren't making significant progress toward the success you want or if you have achieved success on the outside but don't feel secure on the inside, your mental iPod tunes will be self-critical and fearful—an added "oomph" to your daily dose of stress. Without intending to, many of us "get in our own way," causing ourselves stress. And self-imposed stress can be the toughest to get rid of! In Section III, you will learn how to change your perspective, change your physiology, and actually change the problem of the tunes on your mental iPod so you can go through your days confident and fearless.

Make no mistake: There's a clear connection between your level of confidence and your level of stress. The stress of self-doubt is essentially a gap between how you evaluate yourself now and how you want to view yourself and experience your life. This gap can manifest as hammering self-criticism, comparison to others, the constant need to please or "what if . . ." scenario planning: "What if I fail?" "What if I can't figure it out?" "What if I can't bring in more business?" "What if the client doesn't think I'm worth the fee?" Or, it may lurk in the background only to rear its ugly head after you decide that you said something "stupid" in a meeting.

This gap creates chronic frustration and an ever-present pressure to close it. Your ongoing need to "manage the gap" creates stress. For example, if you don't receive any feedback about a presentation, you might worry that "no news is bad news." You might take the lack of feedback personally. Or maybe you feel the need to keep re-doing a project until it's perfect, even though the final 10% improvement soaked up hours of your time, exhausted you, and may have resulted in a missed deadline on another project (none of which made any real difference in the work you delivered).

This is where knowing that you're caught in Survival under Stress cycle can be illuminating. Those negative thoughts have an explanation: Your self-doubt sets up a tense uncertainty within you. Do I have what it takes? Am I good enough? Your stress system crewmembers will work relentlessly to resolve the uncertainty one way or another. If you are not secure in your own sense of worth, you will look outside of yourself for answers to these questions. That's why what your boss or client says (or doesn't say) to you is so important.

In the New Normal, everyone else is too overwhelmed to give you the kind of thoughtful appreciation you richly deserve for all your hard work. And, the higher up you go in the organization and in your field, the less directly you hear positive reinforcement from people above you. The only way out of self-imposed stress is to find a way to deal with your fears and access a source of confidence from within.

If you are like the thousands of people I've counseled, you wish you'd shed these behaviors years ago. You may have tried to "get out of your own way," but after many attempts and only incremental gains, you wonder in private, "Is this just who I am?" Your stress system crewmembers have been broadcasting the same negative messages for so many years that your captain (the conscious, thinking part of you) may have come to believe they are true. The fear of what other people think may be so familiar that you've come to think of it as "part of life."

In Section III, you will learn something my clients learn early on—just how extensively their self-doubts interfere with their productivity. Even a small pocket of self-doubt can curtail your creativity, cost you hours each week, and prevent you from approaching people who could help you succeed. It's exhausting! Remember that highly confident individuals are more productive; they're also often more prosperous. They manage work more efficiently, think more strategically, and have been shown to feel more in control of their ability to fulfill financial goals.[1] Together we will take a look "under the hood" to understand how doubt, perfectionism, and fear can stifle success. You will learn a handful of specific strategies to clear away these barriers and build confidence once and for all! You will learn from the examples of my clients who have used these methods to land bigger-than-ever deals, get promotions faster, and find peace of mind. And, of course, you'll learn how you can too!

6

The Fastest Way to Build Confidence

"I was always looking outside myself for strength and confidence, but it comes from within. It is there all the time."
—ANNA FREUD

Often, people's well-intended effort to increase their own self-confidence actually slows their career progress and prevents the development of the rock solid confidence they seek. Could this be true for you? For an answer, let's draw upon psychology research I conducted at Harvard Medical School for 10 years.

How We Self-Impose Stress

Call it what you will—"secure," "at peace," "whole," "in your zone"—everyone wants an end-state of what I call "confidence at the core." This end point ("Point B" in Figure 6.1) corresponds to how you feel when you are at your Horizon Point (see Chapter 3).

Point A represents your current self-evaluation. This is where any doubts would be portrayed—for instance, if despite a long list of accomplishments and validation from others, you still question or doubt your abilities. You can tell that you have doubts if you, even occasionally, beat yourself up, blame yourself, fear what others think, or call yourself some variation of "idiot." Your "confidence-at-the-

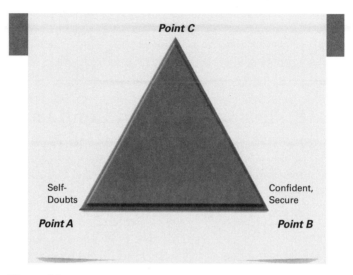

Figure 6.1

core" end-state—the kind of person you could be if free of such doubts —resides at Point B. The distance between Point A and Point B represents the gap between how you evaluate yourself now and the person you want to be.

As human beings, when we are not at Point B, we develop behaviors to get there via Point C ("Other People"), which means we're expending more effort than necessary.

Figure 6.2 illustrates how we waste our time, energy, and attention by involving others in our efforts to feel confident at the core. (How exhausting!) You create a scenario in which you devote time and attention to things that are not within your control, such as what other people think of you. And, as we know from our 50% model, that creates stress.

See if you recognize yourself (or people you work or live with) in these two common types of behaviors.

Type I: Approval Seeking Behavior

If you doubt yourself, you may put a lot of effort into pleasing "Other People" (moving up the left side of the triangle) so they'll think well

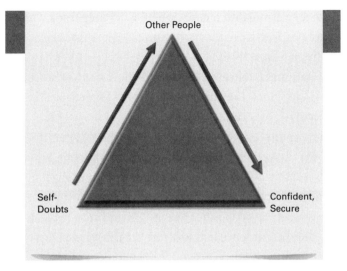

Figure 6.2

of you (top of the triangle). By doing this, you hope to get their approval (moving down the right side of the triangle) (see Figure 6.3).

When others show approval, by complimenting your work for example, you can try to convince yourself, "Well if they think I do a

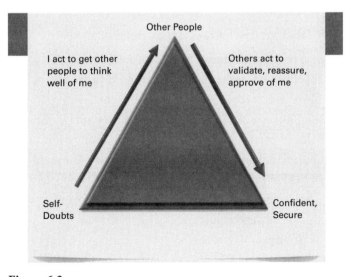

Figure 6.3

good job, then I must do a good job." Or, "If they think I'm worthy, then I must be worthy." This type of thinking provides a shot of confidence, but it's short lived.

This pattern is reflected in many behaviors. Review the list in Chart 6.1 and check the column—"Never," "Sometimes" or "Often" —that best describes you.

Review your scores carefully. If you checked "Often" for three or more of the above behaviors, you qualify as someone who exhibits approval-seeking behavior. Behaviors that you engage in "Sometimes" may reflect either a generous approach to interacting with others and a degree of "political savvy," or they may indicate you are trying to build confidence in a way that creates stress. Do a gut check to determine how much stress you feel when doing these behaviors.

When we first met Stacy, she exhibited a handful of these behaviors: she was a perfectionist who said "yes" when she wanted to say "no." She overprepared for meetings, micromanaged situations, and gave endlessly of herself without expecting anything in return. Stacy's self-imposed pressure resulted in sleepless nights. Even when she got compliments, she shrugged them off without allowing the positive reinforcement to accumulate.

Type II: Disapproval Preventing Behavior

This second pattern illustrates behaviors intended not to gain other people's approval, but rather to prevent their disapproval. As you can see in Figure 6.4, people who exhibit this behavior pattern have doubts about how smart, capable, or worthy they are (as shown in the lower left-hand corner of the diagram). The motivation (as shown moving up the left-hand side of the triangle) is to prevent others from discovering these perceived flaws or deficits. It's important that no one else knows about these doubts, lest they lose respect (down the right-hand side of the triangle).

The reasoning is that when we give significant weight to others' opinions, their critical feedback could be personally deflating. Such a

BEHAVIOR	NEVER	SOMETIMES	OFTEN
I try to please others by figuring out what they want to hear from me instead of sharing my true thoughts.			
I ask other people for their opinions and seek their reassurance, even when I'm qualified to make a decision on my own,			
I say yes to requests when I'd like to say no.			
I "overcomplicate" and "overprepare" for meetings hoping everyone has a good impression of me.			
I feel resentful after I spend time helping other people, particularly when they don't show appreciation for my efforts and advice.			
When speaking in public, I worry about what other people will think of me.			
When I compliment people, I'm "fishing" for return compliments from them.			
I overtalk in the hope that people will think I'm smart.			
I micromanage my team.			
I maneuver to take credit for wins and get recognized by others.			
I spend a lot of time putting "finishing touches" on emails and projects so that people who are in a position to evaluate me will think well of me.			
I feel intimidated when interacting with difficult people.			
I worry and fuss over how I look.			
I go out of my way to help others, even if it leaves me without the time or energy to take care of myself.			
I talk about how I have been a victim so that people will pity me and give me their attention.			
I second guess what others want me to say.			
I give without asking for anything in return.			
TOTAL			

Chart 6.1

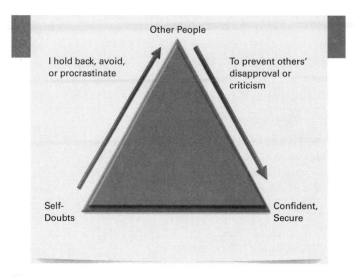

Figure 6.4

negative emotional downward spiral would certainly interfere with achieving the end-state of confidence at the core.

In short, if we believe that we're not good enough or that we don't have what it takes, these disapproval-preventing behaviors will ensure that no one else knows! The best self-protection from negative feedback is simply to avoid it. You think, "I've come up with what may be a good idea, but I'm not sure. If I don't put myself out there, then they can't criticize me! I'll just deny them the opportunity to reject me." With this approach, it's true that you often spare yourself negative emotions by controlling other people's ability to respond to you. But, in doing this, you create stress for yourself by stirring up fear and regret—and it could even stifle your career growth.

Chart 6.2 gives some examples of Type 2 behavior. Do you recognize yourself in any of them? As before, check the label that best describes you.

Again, review your scores. If you checked off three or more of the above as behaviors that you do "Often," you qualify as someone who exhibits this pattern of trying to build confidence in a way that self-

BEHAVIOR	NEVER	SOMEWHAT	OFTEN
I keep quiet and don't speak up in meetings, even when I have something valuable to say.			
I talk about doing things that are essential for my business growth (e.g., starting a blog, working with a coach) but then I procrastinate.			
I'm afraid of looking stupid, so I don't ask for help when I need it.			
I'm reluctant to "put myself out there" by volunteering for a stretch assignment or putting my hat in the ring for a promotion.			
I sell myself short on fees, don't ask for business, or don't negotiate a raise when merited.			
I stay in my comfort zone, calling on lower revenue clients or prospects instead of investing time with A-list clients and asking for referrals to people who can pay my fee.			
I stay busy with familiar tasks, play it safe, and stick with the status quo, avoiding opportunities for innovation or bold leadership lest I'm judged.			
I avoid confrontations because I'm concerned people won't like me, will leave me, or will be angry with me.			
I avoid choosing a target market or differentiating myself in the marketplace because I'm worried I'll alienate prospects.			
I avoid following up even if I know I made a good first impression. If the person gets to know me better, they'll realize how much I don't know!			
I tolerate other people's substandard performance, even putting the blame on myself.			
I don't bring partners or subject matter experts with me to client meetings because I'm threatened by their expertise. (After all, what if the client thinks I don't know my stuff?)			
I soft pedal or couch everything I say, always trying to make others feel better.			
TOTAL			

Chart 6.2

imposes stress. For behaviors that you do "Somewhat," you want to learn the skills to overcome that behavioral block.

You may exhibit behaviors from both the approval-seeking as well as the disapproval-preventing lists or you may be more oriented toward only one of the patterns. As you continue to learn more about these behaviors (and how to leave self-confidence stress behind), bear in mind some of the behaviors that you identified as doing "Often." Most of the strategies in this section are applicable to both behavior patterns. But be on the lookout for those that are specific to one type or the other.

And if it feels like I'm "in your head" or know too much about you, it's because (1) I see these behaviors in my clients all the time and (2) I used to exhibit lots of them myself! Our combined experiences provide "insider information" on how to move past these self-imposed stress behaviors.

Indirect Path Behaviors

When you review Figures 6.1 to 6.4 and your own list of behaviors, you may begin to see that you're on an *Indirect Path* from Point A to Point B (via Point C). Indirect path behaviors are problematic. You would be justified to ask, "If these behaviors get me compliments and prevent me from being criticized, what's the problem? They sound like a good strategy to me!" In the end these well-intended behaviors will cause you stress and thwart your progress. As you already know, **you have the least control over other people's behavior.** Therefore, these behaviors put you on the Survival under Stress cycle and keep you there by:

• **Wasting your time.** How much of your time and attention is wasted on trying to manage other people instead of getting the results you want? C'mon, get out the calculator and add it up. For many of you it could be hours a week—or even per day. That's exhausting!

- **Wasting your energy.** These behaviors serve up short-term, quick fixes. They help you get a compliment or avoid negative feedback in the moment. But, like a sugar high, you must repeat them over and over to keep getting the effect. When other people approve (or don't get the chance to disapprove), you experience momentary elation. But by giving so much weight to other people's opinions, you put them in charge of your emotional state, which is why you feel so "jerked around" and why it feels so important to prevent criticism. Your concerns about other people's views trigger your stress response system, which means you'll use "indirect path" behaviors again to restore your confidence.

- **Providing false confidence.** On some level your caring behaviors are intended to try to control other people's behavior toward you. (For those of you who identify as "people pleasers," brace yourself for this next point. Are you sitting down?) Though you have good intentions, you give to other people so you'll get back a response that will boost your confidence. You give to get. This is similar to not speaking up in meetings. If you are quiet, you're controlling other people's behavior toward you by denying them the opportunity to criticize you.

- **Throwing you off the track.** Most important, the indirect path is the longest route to get to Point B (your sense of confidence and security). In fact, have you ever actually arrived at your destination? Do you have the kind of success and ease you've always sought? On the contrary, you probably still doubt and judge yourself for not making as much progress as you wish you had. You may have outward success, but not an inward sense of security to match. The indirect path has kept you on the Survival Under Stress cycle!

At the beginning of the chapter, I mentioned that your well-intended efforts to build confidence can backfire and even self-impose an extra layer of stress. Now you see why.

Go Direct!

The antidote to the Indirect Path approach is, of course, to Go Direct from Point A to Point B (see Figure 6.5).

When you Go Direct, you cut out the middle person. You alter your approach and source your confidence from within. You don't have to involve others. Therefore, you won't cause yourself stress from trying to control others. Go Direct is based on being impeccable for your 50%. You focus on building your own confidence and prove yourself in your own mind. It's like transitioning from the ups and downs of a sugar cycle to the sustained energy of a protein diet.

Here are three key strategies to shift your perspective so you can Go Direct.

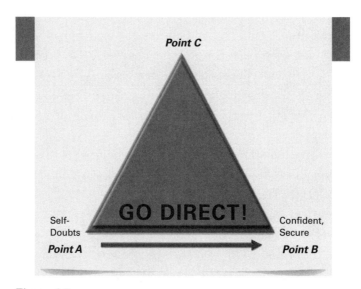

Figure 6.5

1. Build Confidence for the Long Term via Accomplishments, Not Approval

You worry about other people's evaluation because you perceive that you haven't yet proven yourself. **The only way to believe you've**

proven yourself is to create tangible results in the real world. Instead of putting your efforts into achieving quick fixes and momentary approval or the relief of avoiding negative feedback, Go Direct! Put your efforts into meaningful results you can quantify, look back on, and feel proud of. Give to others in ways that you'll remember. When you're engaged, your work brings rewards in and of itself.

The Go Direct approach may result in less immediate complimentary feedback. You have to learn to trust yourself in order to know how you're doing in the meantime (see Chapter 8 for strategies to build self-trust). Ironically, **as soon as you stop trying to get other people's approval, you start producing results that compel them to be impressed with your contribution!**

When you worry about what other people will think, it can set off the stress response cycle led by your SNS crewmembers. You're oriented to think only about yourself and the way others see you, which leads to overthinking, self-doubt, and insecurity. Instead, cultivate behavior that enables you to execute for the long term, not the short term. Think about who you want to be at your Horizon Point, the results you really want to create—and then put your efforts into creating daily progress toward those results.

Stacy saw great results once she began to transform her Indirect Path behaviors into a Go Direct approach. Here's what she did:

- Calmed her frenetic, perfectionist state using three-part breath.
- Clarified her role to do only the right work.
- Built time into her schedule for bigger picture thinking.
- Dealt with, instead of avoiding, a performance issue that was dragging her into the weeds.
- Acted with intention toward her Horizon Point as she went about her day.

These measures gave Stacy the confidence and strategic thinking capacity to come up with a longer term plan to improve the workflow for her team as well as the other two teams under her boss's leadership. No longer did she wait in misery for her boss to propose a re-structure. Instead, she herself submitted a reorganization plan—and her boss accepted it. Then she was promoted to lead all three teams. Stacy, you go girl!

Here is another classic example of a client who advanced in his career on an accelerated timeline using the Go Direct approach.

When Simon came to me, his position at a private equity firm was no longer secure because he hadn't brought in a significant deal in two years. Anxious, he concerned himself with monitoring senior management's evaluations of him. In meetings, he was reluctant to express his convictions and tried to second guess the deals they wanted him to go after. He held back making phone calls to the key connectors in his field out of fear that he didn't have much to offer.

Through our meetings Simon recognized himself in the Indirect Path pattern, and he began to Go Direct! He scheduled "connect-the-dots" time to learn more and started having regular meetings with leaders in his field to deepen his long-term relationships with them. He convened a forum on technology in his field. Soon he had the confidence to share his insights in firm-wide meetings. Though sales cycles in his industry are usually 18 months, he closed the second biggest deal in the firm's history—in just four months! Let's just say Simon's job is more secure now.

Build confidence through accomplishments and not through other people's perceptions. What are your ideas and plans to build accomplishments for the long term in order to Go Direct?

_____

_____

_____

2. Focus on the End User

Want a good strategy for taking the attention away from you? Try putting it on the "end user" of your work. The end user is the person or group that will use or benefit from your efforts. If you're writing a report, the end user could be your boss or someone else who will implement your recommendations. If you're in business for yourself, your end users vary—from prospects and strategic partners to your clients and all the people whose lives your product or service will ultimately improve.

If you're a worrier and know you won't be able to break that habit anytime soon, try worrying about the right things! Instead of wondering what people think of you, put your effort into understanding your end users' needs—and use that as motivation to improve your impact on them. Think about how they'll benefit from the intervention that you have an opportunity to make right now. In the words of Mahatma Gandhi, "The best way to find yourself is to lose yourself in the service of others."

For example, whenever I sit down to write a presentation, even before my fingertips hit the keyboard, the first thing I do is think about what I want the participants to walk away with. I ask myself, "How can I best convey the information so they will be able to use it immediately in their lives?" And, whenever I'm asked to speak without notes in front of a large audience, I shift my attention away from my jittery nerves by thinking about the skills I'm about to impart to the end users (the audience). That puts my captain back in charge, and reminds me to trust myself that I have something of value to say. (Remember, even the *illusion* of control puts us on the Success Under Stress cycle!)

Similarly, when I have an initial consultation with potential clients to determine if my services are a good fit for their needs, I don't focus on whether I'm going to sell them or if I'm worth my fee. Those are Indirect Path concerns. Instead, I listen carefully to what they want and create a mental picture of the skill building we'll go through together. I picture the confidence, balance, and progress this potential client could have within weeks of our conversation. I imagine everyone who will be positively affected by their improvement. Then I describe the specific steps we would do together, which gives the person the necessary information to determine whether my services are the right fit. I aim to make the discussion valuable in and of itself. It's all about the results they could get, not about regulating my self-esteem.

Here's how you speak up. I met Monique after my talk at Working Mother's Multicultural Women's Conference. She's an HR professional at a large restaurant, responsible for the policies that affect workers. "I was invited to a meeting with senior management," she told me, "and I had solid knowledge of the impact policy changes would have. I wanted to speak up, but I froze. I had all these doubts running through my mind: Would they think my comments were stupid?" Notice that Monique's concerns were related to herself and to the moment. They were about the "small game," such as how her comments would be perceived. Had she spoken up she could have gone after the "big game" of serving her end users—the millions of workers in their restaurants around the world. Her comments could have had lasting impact, they might have been implemented into HR policy—but she didn't speak up.

By being purposeful and having a strong guiding sense of passion about the contribution you can make to your end users, you can drown out your personal concerns. Make the issue about your contribution, not about the moment.

Think of a situation in which you lack confidence. Who are your end users, and how can you Go Direct to address their needs?

_____

_____

_____

3. Practice a "Do-It-Yourself" Model

Becoming who you want to be at your Horizon Point and acting in the service of that person is a continuous process. Once you commit, you'll experience a deep state of satisfaction as you live up to your own standards and "do the right thing," even when your colleagues, bosses, or clients fail to acknowledge it.

The boomerang effect of Indirect Path behaviors is formed naturally and normally through the feedback of parents, teachers, siblings, and friends as we're growing up. The process of becoming an adult involves learning to get that feedback from within, relying on others' input less and less.

Sara, a participant in my online Fast Confidence program, was a consultant who had to write reports for her clients. Though a seasoned professional with twenty years in the business, she thought she wasn't smart enough. She doubted whether her work was as good as her competitors'. She'd spin her wheels for hours, poring over the drafts and asking her colleagues for feedback. To Go Direct, she developed more objectivity so she could look at her reports relative to their intended purpose rather than how they reflected on her. Instead of worrying, "What will they think of me?," she asked herself questions, such as: "Did I make the necessary points?" or "If I take a step back and read this report for the first time, will it seem clear?" Cutting out the middle person freed up an average of five hours every week!

Start acting in the service of the person who fulfills your Horizon Point, and you will quickly become that person. Back in Chapter 3, I introduced you to the story of Pamela, a junior partner at a big four consulting firm. Though she had a weak reputation and was not perceived as a leader (in fact, feedback about her was that she was "mousy"), she had a Horizon Point of "Confident Leader." Before she acted, she would ask whether her behavior served her Horizon Point. As a result, she began to spend less time on technical emails and more on developing her team members. Soon, she felt more comfortable speaking up with strategic recommendations in her C-suite meetings. She showed confidence and let her division head know of her ambitions. Six months later she was put in charge of the regional office and, shortly thereafter, assigned to an international decision-making body. All because she stopped looking for recognition from her colleagues and began making contributions worthy of her desired position!

If you're wondering whether I'm advising you not to care what anyone else thinks of you, the answer is No! You should be cognizant of feedback from your boss and colleagues in order to be a more effective team player and develop yourself professionally and personally. And, of course, you should seek feedback on client satisfaction and how you could improve your services. The question is whether you have a solid base of confidence from which you can reliably draw your self-evaluation—or whether you must divert your time and energy into deriving that evaluation exclusively from other people. Once you have a base of confidence, you can hear feedback objectively and filter it as information about your performance and/or the situation, not about you or your worth as a person!

When you're confident in yourself, you're more open to feedback because you want to improve. When you lack confidence, you tend to overscrutinize other people's opinions and weigh them more heavily than your own. You take their feedback personally and respond emotionally, feeling demoralized. Your emotional response interferes with your ability to listen constructively and tweak your work-related behavior. Consequently, you deprive yourself of valuable feedback mechanisms to actually grow your confidence level.

Evaluate Your Behaviors: Indirect Path or Direct Path?

Now that you are aware of the distinction, you can be more conscious of your behaviors and ask yourself if they are Indirect Path or Direct Path. This is nuanced. In some instances, you will see both patterns in the same behavior. For example, imagine you're at a networking event and you talk with someone whom you think is "above your status." Later, you follow up with that person. You try to deliver some value, such as introducing them to someone else or sending them an

THE FASTEST WAY TO BUILD CONFIDENCE 129

article of interest. This response could be a Direct Path behavior if you're motivated by generosity and an effortless inclination to lead by giving first. Or, it could be an Indirect Path behavior if you spend hours of your day trying to figure out how to ingratiate yourself with the higher status person or are anxious to get a response so you can feel special. Here's one way to know: Do a gut check. Does the follow-up feel effortless? Did the initial conversation feel natural, expansive and energetic—or "icky?" Are you acting in service of the person you want to be at your Horizon Point or are you angling for validation? Once you become aware of the motivation behind your Indirect Path behaviors, they begin to hold less appeal and even signal upcoming disappointment. From the very first time you practice a Go Direct approach, you'll feel proud, and you will likely see a win. Then, reinforced to do it again next time, you'll soon find yourself on the Success Under Stress cycle.

In sum, Indirect Path behaviors soak up your time, energy and attention. When you Go Direct, you free up time, make a better contribution and earn more money. You build confidence from within, from the fruits of your own accomplishments. Acting in the service of creating value and building long-term relationships always trumps a "quick fix" (which only leads you to need to seek reassurance again). Now that's the kind of plan your captain would devise—one that puts you on the Success Under Stress cycle.

What is your Go Direct approach?

_____

_____

_____

_____

_____

_____

ACTION PLAN

- Complete the checklists of Indirect Path behaviors and note whether you fit the pattern(s) of Approval Seeking and/or Disapproval Preventing Behaviors.
- Take a situation in which you are currently using Indirect Path behaviors and Go Direct! Choose one or more of the three Go Direct strategies and make a plan for how you can use that strategy to Go Direct in the situation.
- Get feedback and write your success story in the community forum at www.sharonmelnick.com.

POINTS TO REMEMBER

To the extent that we doubt ourselves, we set up a behavior pattern in which we manage other people's perceptions in an attempt to build our self-confidence. However, these behaviors interfere with building self-confidence by wasting time, energy, and attention. These patterns are known as "indirect path" behaviors—because of the way they approach your own sense of confidence, that is, Seeking Other's Approval or Preventing Others' Disapproval.

The antidote to indirect-path behaviors is to Go Direct!

Three helpful ways to shift perspective are:

- Build confidence for the long term via accomplishments, not approval.
- Focus on fulfilling the needs of your end user, not on managing others' perceptions.
- Practice a "Do-It-Yourself" model in which you build your own confidence from within by putting your efforts into becoming the person you defined at your Horizon Point.

Recommended Resources

- Go to www.sharonmelnick.com for videos and resources on how to Go Direct.

7

Quick Fixes to Eliminate Anxiety

"You can't wring your hands and roll up your sleeves at the same time."
—PAT SCHROEDER, *U.S. Congresswoman*

Many of the stresses that we attribute to our emotional state—such as feeling anxious, having low self-regard, or being reactive—stem from our physiology. These so-called "false moods"[1] occur because we lack the brain chemistry to support resilience to stress. But there's good news: these states can change quickly, as we change our physiology.

I asked Harvard integrative medicine specialist Sara Gottfried, MD, how we can avoid feeling as though we've failed if we don't live up to Superwoman or Superman standards every minute of the day. She suggested a new mantra: "It's my adrenals, it's not me." According to Gottfried, we need to stop blaming and pressuring ourselves and instead begin to "get curious about our biology."[2]

So, let's follow the doctor's orders. But before I guide you toward the biology you want to create to get on the Success Under Stress cycle, I want to share a few secret weapons for an immediate confidence boost and anxiety reduction.

Quick Fixes for Anxiety and Self-Doubt

Part of achieving Success Under Stress is gaining control over getting into—and staying in—a confident state, no matter what's happening around you. Here are some practical tools you can use with notice-able impact.

However, to understand the toolbox of exercises presented here, I asked Joseph Michael Levry, PhD, founder of Naam Yoga Therapies, to explain how pressing acupressure points on your hands can give you a beneficial result. He replied:

> Folding the fingers of the hands in different postures and hold-ing them for specific periods causes a healing pressure to be applied on particular nerves. These hand and finger postures can generate various qualities such as fearlessness, confidence, power and peace in the practitioner, and can provide healing effects for various health problems. In the fingertips of every human being, there are many concentrated nerve root end-ings, which are free energy discharge points. By touching to-gether the tips of the fingers or the finger tips to other parts of the hand, the 'life force' is redirected back into the body along veins, tendons, glands, sensory organs and back up to the brain, thus balancing basic elements of the body.[3]

In effect, you have access to an internal pharmacy.

TOOL #1: *The Panic Reset Button*

If you, like so many people, become nervous before presenting or speaking in public, use the following acupressure point, which I call the "Panic Reset" button.

TOOL #1 The "Panic Reset"

Hand Position: Touch your thumb to the knuckle on the side of your middle (third) finger. Then move your thumb back toward your palm, feeling for a "soft" spot or a slight indentation in between. Apply medium pressure there.

According to neuroscientist Sonia Sequeira, PhD, this spot touches a point . . . that correlates to a nerve that runs from the chest to the tip of the middle finger. The meridian is related to your heart area. When you apply pressure to that point it helps to regulate blood pressure and reduce anxiety.

TOOL #2: *The Confidence Point*

For a boost of confidence, try pressing the Confidence Point button. According to Sequeira: "You are applying pressure to a meridian that corresponds to a nerve related to the function of the large intestine, which has subtle energy related to having charisma and feeling powerful, or its opposite."[4] When you press this point it sends signals that reduce internal emotional commotion and induce a state that is subtly more confident. Place your hands in this position for as few as 30 seconds before you speak up in a presentation, or whenever you need a shot of confidence.

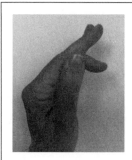

TOOL #2   The "Confidence Point"

Hand Position: Use either hand to touch your thumb to the side of the index finger in between the first and second knuckles. Apply mild to moderate pressure.

TOOL #3: *The Push-Away-Fear Breath*

You can train your body to get rid of fear. Try this exercise, also from Naam Yoga. The vigorous exhale stimulates your PNS, helping to create calm. I've used this breath to dampen my claustrophobia so that I can live with less stress in New York City, where crowded subways and elevators are a part of life!

TOOL #3   "Push-Away-Fear Breath"

Breath: Breathe in through your nose and out through your mouth vigorously, with an accentuated inhale and exhale. Each time you breathe out, forcefully push your hands away from you (like you are pushing away something you don't want) and exhale through your mouth. Then breathe in through your nose and bring your hands back in a straight line toward your chest, with your elbows by your side. Then breathe out vigorously through your mouth, again pushing away your hands. Repeat.

Hand Position: Bring together the tips of the thumb and index finger and bring your hands up so they are in front of your chest facing away from you.

Duration: Start doing this exercise for one minute and work your way up to three minutes. It may make you feel a little lightheaded the first few times; just stop if it feels uncomfortable.

TOOL #4: *Problem-Solving Position*

To Go Direct (as discussed in Chapter 6), you must build your self-trust and consult your intuition to solve problems. Here is a hand position you can use to activate your brain's problem-solving center. It draws focus to a point on your forehead that corresponds to the approximate location of your pineal gland, which is at the intersection of your left and right hemisphere and provides access to "whole brain thinking." Some spiritual and physical yoga traditions refer to this as the "third eye," the seat of intuition and wisdom.

In this position you're symbolically connecting the centers that are involved with intuition (right hand) and "gut instincts" (left hand). Now your head and your gut can "communicate" with each other!

TOOL #4   Problem-Solving Position

Hand Position: Place the fingertips of your *right* hand in the position of your thumb touching the fingertips of your 2nd (index) and 3rd (middle) fingers. Place the "tip" of that triangle shape about 1 inch away from the point on your forehead, which is about 1 inch above the point that is directly between your eyes.

Simultaneously, place the fingertips of your *left* hand in that same position of your thumb touching the fingertips of your 2nd (index) and 3rd (middle) fingers. Place the "tip" of that triangle shape about an inch away from the point that would correspond to your "gut."

Balance Your Stress System to Help You Be More Confident and Less Irritable

Around the lunch table at a training for a women's leadership network, the women on my left were earnestly sharing tips on how to set the tone for leading through upcoming layoffs. They were also joyfully sharing stories of their latest passions, which included yoga and cooking. I smiled like a proud parent at their resilience. Then, I turned to the three women on my right. Like many others with whom I talk, they were sharing war stories—in this case about over-the-counter remedies for infections, exhaustion, sleeplessness, headaches, and "feeling blah." It didn't seem to occur to any of them that they shouldn't have to endure these physical hardships. In fact, there are easy, immediately accessible steps you can take to restore your stress system and your health.

Up to 70% of people who are stressed out have some form of adrenal imbalance (referring to those walnut shaped adrenal glands that produce the hormones underlying your response to stress.)[5] Un-

QUICK FIXES TO ELIMINATE ANXIETY   137

der chronic stress, our bodies go through three stages that form a deteriorating spectrum of adrenal imbalance and, then, depletion.

In the first stage, we muster up the extra energy to deal with stressors. After the initial shot of adrenaline we read about in Chapter 4, the adrenals pump out cortisol, which at first—and in short bursts—provides strength and stamina. At the right levels, cortisol helps metabolize food, fight allergies, and reduce inflammation. But when our high-alert state continues over time, our glands pump too much adrenaline and cortisol, thereby depleting our "feel good" neurotransmitters, such as serotonin (which helps you feel self-confident and optimistic), and dopamine (which helps you feel pleasure). In fact, when cortisol circulates chronically in our systems, it actually fuels inflammation and can cause the very diseases it was intended to prevent. Consequently, we begin to see signs of illness or infections. No longer will we experience that "high" from the adrenaline rush; instead, we feel flat or even depressed. Too little or too much may result in a lack of attention, a feeling of being overwhelmed or, as Gottfried suggests, "that 'I just can't get that same focus I used to have' feeling."[6] We reach for external remedies, such as caffeine or salty or sugary foods. We push ourselves even harder at exercise or, do the reverse, we stop exercising.[7] This sets us up to feel chronically wired and tired.

To describe the most advanced stage of adrenal imbalance, I turned to Marcelle Pick, RNC, MSN, OB/GYN Nurse Practitioner and Cofounder of the Women to Women's healthcare clinic: "In the final Exhaustion phase," she explained, "our adrenals are so compromised that they can't produce enough of their stress hormones. Every little problem starts to seem like a major disaster, when your son spilling his milk or your boss giving you a disapproving look feels like the end of the world."[8]

We've all been there—from time to time. But if this is your normal state, your system may be in danger of adrenal burnout. There are things all of us do to exacerbate this adrenal imbalance without necessarily knowing it. "A high-sugar, low-protein diet can trigger stress reactions without our even realizing it,"[9] according to best-selling author and nutritionist Julia Ross. Ironically, over 70% of us eat the very worst junk foods in order to relieve our emotional stress.[10]

Everyone should get their stress hormone levels tested so they know where they fit on the adrenal depletion continuum (because you can't necessarily tell from your "symptoms.") For example, if you're fatigued, it may be due to either high or low cortisol (though with low cortisol you'll feel weak and tired, while with high cortisol you'll feel tired but irritable). According to Gottfried, "We tend to know our 401(k) numbers but not our cortisol levels" and urges us to "manage our neurohormonal dashboard as aggressively as a retirement plan."[11]

The bottom line is that you don't have to feel worn down, anxious, or sick from stress. Instead of pushing through your signs of stress or low-grade feelings of anxiety (and then judging yourself for it), remember to be "impeccable for your 50%!" Start with the strategies in this book to have more balance and less emotional stress while learning about your physiology. There are many easy ways to do this. For example, you can start with a self-assessment using the Recommended Resources at the end of this chapter. There's a saliva-based test you can purchase yourself or your healthcare provider can order a blood test and help you understand the results. Then, you can reset your adrenal levels with the right mix of natural or prescribed remedies.

Marcelle Pick advises starting with nutritional changes, then seeing what improvements you begin to notice.[12] If you're experiencing adrenal imbalance, this approach will give you a good idea of the cause—and you can begin to restore your adrenal health within 30 days. Start with small, consistent changes to your nutrition (such as a high-protein, gluten-free, and vegetable diet), take natural vitamins and supplements (more B-complex and Omega 3–fish oil, for example), and try out a host of natural herbs (e.g., rhodiola for concentration and balance; chamomile or passion flower to boost the "calming" parts of your brain; cordyceps, and ashwagandha).

I urge you to check out the Recommended Resources at the end of this chapter and—if applicable—customize a plan to reverse the trend of your adrenal imbalance. Start feeling fantastic again soon!

ACTION PLAN

- Tools #1, #2, and #4 are best applied in the moment you need them. The breathing technique in Tool #3 can be used in the "heat of the moment," yet will give maximum effect when practiced on a regular basis.
- Ask your doctor for a screen of adrenal-related markers. Consult the recommended resources below to learn what your scores mean and, next, take the steps as advised by a healthcare professional.

POINTS TO REMEMBER

- We face a near universal condition of imbalance from the output of our adrenal gland stress response. Depending on where you are in the process of adrenal imbalance, you may experience signs of energy depletion, anxiety, or depression. You may have symptoms that cause unnecessary suffering (such as "brain fog" or difficult sleeping).
- Get your stress hormone levels checked so you can put together a personalized plan to restore the balance of your adrenal levels and experience again a sense of confidence and fearlessness.
- Tools to change your physiology include:

  "Panic Reset"
  "Confidence Point"
  "Push-Away-Fear Breath"
  "Problem-Solving Position"

Recommended Resources

- M. Pick, *Are You Tired and Wired: Your Proven 30-day Program for Overcoming Adrenal Fatigue and Feeling Fantastic Again.*[12] www.womentowomen.com, cofounded by M. Pick, includes an encyclopedic array of articles, resources, quizzes, and other helpful tools to find out where you are on the spectrum of adrenal imbalance, what type of adrenal profile you have, and what kind of diet and lifestyle changes you can easily make to reverse any damage that is leading to stress signs in your mood and energy level.
- S. Gottfried, *The Hormone Cure: Reclaim Balance, Sleep, Sex Drive, and Vitality With the Gottfried Protocol.* (New York: Scribner/ Simon & Schuster, forthcoming 2013) or go to her sassy, inspiring, and highly informative website: www.saragottfriedmd.com
- J. B. Ross, (2003) *The Mood Cure: The 4-Step Program to Take Charge of Your Emotions.*[1]

8

Techniques for Turning Self-Criticism into Self-Confidence

"What lies before me, and what lies behind me, are tiny matters compared to what lies within me"
—RALPH WALDO EMERSON

One of the questions I hear most often from people who attend my training seminars is, "How can I get rid of negative thinking and overcome the fear of failure?" That's what Stacy and Dan wanted to know too! See if you can relate.

Stacy's "mental iPod" sounded like this: "I always feel that I have to be the one to do it all, and perfectly. I question myself obsessively. I kill myself over things, yet it always turns out I do a great job. I worry I'll say the wrong thing, so I second guess myself. And then if I don't say anything, I think, 'You missed an opportunity, you are such an idiot!' If I continue along this pattern I'll fail at being satisfied in my life."

Dan told me he had tremendous financial goals, "but I'm not reaching them. I feel like a failure. Self-assurance, that's what I need. I want to be less fearful about what other people think of me. I want to walk into the room and be respected."

Here are several ways to turn self-criticism into self-confidence.

Be a Better DJ of Your Own "Mental iPod"

In earlier chapters, I introduced the idea that 60,000 thoughts a day stream through your mind and that your inner self-talk is like a mental iPod. It's the soundtrack of your life—motivating or deflating, depending on the playlist. Many people believe that the best way to motivate themselves is to be harsh and critical. But that's a myth! Try this experiment. Call to mind a typical stressful thought you have. What is that thought and, more important, what is its tone? Is it head banging? Resigned? Anxious? Critical? Try repeating this thought a few times and notice its physical sensations. Tension in your shoulders? Pressure in your head? If you are having those kinds of thoughts thousands of times a week (or even thousands of times a day)—no wonder you come home exhausted. Do these thoughts motivate you?

Often, the way you talk to yourself is the way you talk to others. If you want to inspire people, start by inspiring yourself. Knowing this may also make it easier to be empathetic toward someone else who is very critical. After all, if they're using that harsh tone of voice, they must be equally critical of themselves—if not more so. So, step one is to pay attention to your mental iPod's playlist.

When you're at the gym trying to work out and a song comes on that doesn't motivate you, what do you do? Click. Like a DJ, you change the tune! Similarly, your mental iPod can adopt the voice and tone of someone who respects and appreciates you. Think of someone who believes in you and recall that champion's tone of voice. It's probably different from the one you hammer yourself with. Whenever you have a negative thought, try to reconstruct it through that person's tone of voice. What would they say to you about the same subject? And how would they say it?

Let's practice. Think of a typical negative thought you have—for example: "I'll never get it all done," or, "I can't." Then think of how that encouraging person would talk to you. They'd probably say, "You always get it done in the end, and you really do it well." Once you have an example of a "new phrase in a new tone," repeat your champion's words a few times in your own mind. Use the tone you think your champion would use. Now, what physical sensation does that cause? Thousands of people I've guided through this exercise say they get an immediate feeling of energy, warmth, and expansion. Both Dan and Stacy used it to concentrate on who they wanted to be at their Horizon Points, instead of having their thoughts create stress for them. At www.sharonmelnick.com you can download a 40-minute audio training on how to change your thoughts from negative and stressful to positive and productive by being a better DJ of your mental iPod.

Move Past Doubts That Keep You Stuck

When on the Survival Under Stress cycle, you tend to be subjective, not objective. That's because your SNS crewmembers set you up to see interactions through your own fears and to dwell on what others think about you. A perfect example is the moment you want to speak up in a meeting. You have an idea you think is valuable, but the nervousness wells up within you and the inner debate begins: "Should I say it, or not? Do I know enough? What if they think it's stupid?" This debate keeps you uncertain about how to act. It makes *you* the focus, instead of the meeting. But what if your "playlist" included, "This comment provides important information or perspective." Or what if you could simply click on the tune: "Go for it!" To be more effective, be more objective. Your self-evaluation can be within your own control, not other peoples'. The two-step exercise below will help you get clarity to move past doubts that keep you uncertain about yourself.

Step 1 Identify Your Doubt

Usually your doubt (or perceived weakness) is a vague, high-level conviction about yourself. Examples: "I'm not smart enough," "I'm not as competent as my counterparts," "I could never have the success she's having," and so on. You can't attack a problem if you don't know what it is! So the first step is to take that high-level doubt and break it into its component parts. If you think you aren't "smart enough," what exactly does that mean? That your presentations aren't as articulate as you would like them to be? That you would like to have more creative ideas in brainstorming meetings? That you didn't attend as a prestigious school as your colleagues did? Write down the specific components of your doubt:

_____

_____

_____

Step 2 Decide Whether to ACCEPT or ACCOMPLISH

For each component of your doubt you're going to make a decision: either ACCEPT OR ACCOMPLISH.

* **ACCEPT**—Acknowledge that the perceived weakness is real for you. Choose to concentrate on your strengths and/or find a workaround so that your success doesn't depend on this skill. You decide not to "work on" the "weakness" but rather to accept it.
* **ACCOMPLISH**—You decide that the perceived weakness is mission critical for your success, and you should work to improve the skill. Build the skill into a strength (or at least an area of competence). Make an action plan and build in accountability. The goal is that after a set period of time (weeks or months), this weakness will no longer be an obstacle for you.

Let's look at how Stacy stepped through this exercise. Originally trained as a lawyer and not in the broader business skills, she was self-conscious about her lack of strategic thinking abilities. We discussed whether she could ACCEPT or ACCOMPLISH.

Stacy decided that overall, strategic thinking was critical for her role, so she decided to commit to ACCOMPLISH each of the components. Here's an example of her ACCOMPLISH plan:

- Have proactive meetings with key business partners to understand the wider issues.
- Commit to asking questions: "I am new in this business role and recognize my questions may be a bit basic, but the more I know the better I can provide advice."
- Schedule "connect-the-dots time" to brainstorm possible risk scenarios for presentation to the business partners.

Once Stacy had this plan in place, she knew exactly how to move past the block of self-consciousness about her strategic thinking capabilities. She began working her plan and was quickly able to improve those abilities and not hold back on this mission-critical aspect of taking herself to the next level.

An ACCEPT vs. ACCOMPLISH exercise for whatever doubts you are facing means you won't feel stuck and you won't want to hide. For you, perhaps it makes the most sense to ACCEPT your perceived weaknesses and focus on your strengths. Or, maybe making an action plan to ACCOMPLISH bridging the skill gap will prove more fruitful. Or, your solution could be a combination of the two. It's a matter of what's right for you. You'll know when you've made good choices because you'll feel more energized and at peace.

Another example: Hal is a commercial realtor who feels comfortable with clients who are creative professionals. He feels intimidated showing property to clients who are in financial professions because they are very "numbers oriented," caring less about how the space "feels." Hal needs to increase his business, but he lives in New York City, which has an abundance of finance professionals! He was spinning his wheels—until he made his chart:

ACCEPT	ACCOMPLISH
I'm great with creative professional clients—I choose them as a niche.	Until I establish myself in my new niche, I will ask someone in my office to mentor me on the language to use with financial services clients. I also commit to taking a course in order to know the quantitative piece better.

Hal's commitment to ACCEPT provided huge relief. He found he could be successful by being himself and working with the clients who were creative professionals. To reflect his new niche, he tweaked some of his marketing materials and prioritized meetings with certain referral sources. Result: He had a new commission within three weeks!

Fill out your ACCEPT vs. ACCOMPLISH plan here. Which strategy do you choose?

	ACCEPT	ACCOMPLISH
Doubt #1		
Doubt #2		
Doubt #3		

Q: I manage a team of people who have more technical expertise than me, which makes me self-conscious. What should I do?

A: I recommend two approaches to improve your confidence when you're managing people with more technical expertise than you. First, clarify your role on the team (review Chapter 5, if necessary). Here's how my client Caren, a mid-level manager for a financial technology company, worked out this challenge for herself. She recently made a lateral move to manage a team of IT developers. Her role required her to direct projects and manage timelines, but she didn't need to know the technical skills the coders would use to build the software. She was able to ACCEPT that her role (and her strength) was to manage the team, not to do the actual coding. Her ACCOMPLISH was to gain greater knowledge of their coding language by taking a course, reading more online, and regularly asking the coders to explain the key points she needed to know. After only three weeks of implementing this plan, Caren said, "I have definitely been feeling more confident, and I got kudos after last week's staff meeting in which I gave an update for my team."

Second, shift gears from self-criticism to critical thinking. Stop pressuring yourself to know everything. You don't have to! Indeed, in the New Normal, it's impossible to be on top of every new development. Instead, sharpen your critical thinking skills so you can walk confidently into any situation, even one in which you're new to the topic and less informed than others. That's being impeccable for your 50%. Don't overthink what you don't know, but do get trained in the skills that will prepare you to lead in any situation. (See the Recommended Resources at the end of this chapter.)

Build Self-Trust with an Intuition Log

Try this exercise to build trust in your judgments to get on the Success Under Stress cycle. It will help you remain objective and base your decisions on facts, not doubts.

Start an "Intuition Log" to record how you act in a variety of situations where you must make a decision. This tool will allow you to review your successful and unsuccessful judgments over time and identify patterns that will help you know whether or not you can trust your intuition. Your Intuition Log has three columns: Situation, Your Intuition/What You Did, and Outcome. The first two will be filled out at the time you make the decision or just after. In the first column, record the situation you are/were in. In the second, record what your judgment or intuition tells you to do, and what you end up doing.

Fill out the third column over time, documenting the outcome of the situation and noting whether it was positive and/or whether it validated your judgment. A positive outcome and an outcome that validated your judgment are often similar, but not always. For example, your intuition may have told you that a problem was brewing and that you should speak up about it, but then you didn't. If the problem subsequently "blew up" and could have been averted by your having the courage to notify the responsible parties, it means the outcome was negative, but your intuition was validated.

As the entries grow, begin reviewing them for patterns. Out of your first 10 entries, what was the percentage of time your intuition proved "correct" or "valid?" If you have a pattern in which nine out of ten times your intuition is correct, start paying much closer attention to your "gut instinct." This is especially important if your intuition is right but you act against it. If your intuition is right only five out of ten times, look more closely into each of the situations in which your intuition was off base. You should begin to see patterns: Do you overlook information? Do you consider other people's points of view, but not your own?

Similarly, notice if you have doomsday prophecies that never play out (reminiscent of the French philosopher Michel de Montaigne's quote, "My life has been full of terrible misfortunes most of which never happened.") Your pattern on the Intuition Log can help you put those catastrophic scenarios in perspective. Next time they come up, you won't give them so much credence. You will be too busy using the techniques found in Section III to decrease fear and increase intuition!

Q: What can I do if I fear that I am not doing enough or if I pressure myself too much to succeed?

A: Many emerging leaders tell me they pressure themselves too much to succeed. Fearing failure, they hold themselves back from taking risks and speaking up with their opinions. Let's turn to someone who's been through that fire and came out on the other side to share her wisdom and perspective.

Ana Sanchez is working mother who was promoted twice within a short period of time and is now a senior level leader at a large consumer products company. The first in her family to go to college and have a career, Ana felt pressure to succeed. Early in her career, she says, "I worried that my work wasn't good enough and put way too much pressure on myself. I would end up pushing myself too hard, giving everything 120% when some things don't need 120%." Here are two keys Ana learned for turning what she calls her early "paranoia" into success:

- **Find people you trust and who have more perspective than you—people who are well informed and know the politics.** Someone in front of whom you don't always have to have it all figured out. Establish "sanity checks" along the way that ensure your judgment is sound. And be open to feedback so you'll learn from your mentor's guidance.
- **Learn how to ask questions rather than get caught up in needing to know the answer.** "I couldn't have learned to ask smart questions if I didn't also ask the dumb ones along the way," Ana recalls. "Ask a lot of questions in the beginning and then ask smarter questions over time. You have to push through the discomfort by requiring yourself to have an opinion—knowing there might not be a safety net—and come to the point where you are able to make decisions on your own."

Ana was open to feedback to help her grow. Go Direct is about having enough belief in yourself to be open to feedback without needing the other person to give you confidence. In other words, you can absorb the feedback objectively and not take it personally.

Ask for feedback from your manager, colleagues, or direct reports. If you're a business owner, you can survey your clients and/or your staff. Develop an action plan for putting their feedback into play to help you grow. Marshall Goldsmith's "feedforward" technique has become a gold standard in getting constructive suggestions for how to improve performance in the future rather than rehashing the past.[1]

Free Yourself from the Pressures of Perfectionism

As comedienne Tina Fey wrote in her hilarious memoir *Bossypants*: "Perfect is overrated. The *Saturday Night Live* show we produced was never perfect. Perfect is boring on live television."[2]

Pressure to "do it all"—and to do it all well—is a central theme for many of my clients. Their internal voices are a constant source of pressure and stress. The pressure stops you from pressing the "Off button" that enables you to relax and renew. Your inner voice drives you to attain perfection—whether it's staying up late baking cookies, micromanaging your team to avoid mistakes, or worrying about doing enough on your own projects - and makes you feel guilty if you don't meet your standards. But at what cost?

As with all of the other stress-reduction strategies in this book, it's always helpful to understand why you're driven to behave a certain way and why you're so hard on yourself. In my experience, there are three sources of fuel for perfectionism (and it's helpful to know the source of your perfectionism so you can take actions to tame it):

- **Passion**: Sometimes perfectionism comes from pure passion. Are you a creatively gifted artist with a keen eye for the details of how something should look or the way a message should be communicated?

- **Prevention of Disapproval**: Your perfectionism can be a fear-based attempt to ward off disapproval and loss of "love." My client Jeanine, a senior executive in the fashion industry who is outwardly confident and noted for excellence on the job, described it well:

  It's inherent in the fashion industry to work at a frenetic pace, but I see now that I have an extra oomph of frenetic energy because I am so worried that my team will make a mistake. To someone else a mistake might just be a bad business moment, i.e., we lost some money, our plans were delayed. But I go immediately to thinking it's my fault and take on blame and responsibility. Did I source the fabric wrong? Is it my team's fault? Am I going to end up looking bad? Then I feel this rising pressure to fix it, immediately!

  Jeanine was afraid that she or her team would make a mistake. If that happened, it would be *her* fault. And, if it were her fault, then in her mind it meant she wasn't good enough, that she deserved criticism instead of respect. Like Jeanine, you may fear losing respect in the workplace, but at a deeper emotional level the fear is that you will lose love of people you need in order to source your self-confidence! This source of perfectionism is analogous to the second type of Indirect Path behavior we discussed and found solutions for in Chapter 6.

- **Prepping for Approval**: Some of us harbor the mistaken belief that if only we could be perfect, it would get us the love and approval we hope for—perhaps because we think that people who were important to us when we were growing up gave us their attention based on how worthy we were. So we drive ourselves in a never-ending, never achievable pursuit of perfection. At the time we developed this misconception, we couldn't recognize that the other person's attention was conditional, based on *their* limitations, not ours.

Try to pinpoint the source(s) of your perfectionism so you'll know how to reverse the trend. If your perfectionism comes from passion, know that you might never tame it fully because it's part of the special talent and gift that differentiates you. At the same time, be aware that having this pure passion for the details doesn't excuse you from treating others disrespectfully (causing them to get on the Survival Under Stress cycle!) You also need to cultivate your "Off Button" and find ways of renewing yourself so that you don't burn out.

If the source of perfectionism is prevention of disapproval or prepping for approval, it's related to confidence. These behavior patterns may stem from difficult experiences earlier in life that led you to develop perfectionism because you weren't able to get the love and attention you deserved just for being you.

Stacy's perfectionism came from a confidence issue. She used the strategies I just described to free herself from the pressures of her high standards. Remember: you're the DJ of your mental iPod. So change the tune of your self-talk!. Turn away from self-criticism and toward critical thinking. Distinguish between what's actually expected of you and the unrealistic pressure you're putting on yourself, using the ACCEPT vs. ACCOMPLISH exercise. You can either enjoy the relief that comes from accepting your strengths and/or get busy developing skills so you will no longer see a gap in your abilities. Develop objective self-trust with your Intuition Log so you'll know when a project is "good enough" to hit "send!"

Stacy also used the strategies from Chapter 5 to appreciate her strengths and the value that she could bring to her work and her parenting. Because perfectionism often comes from longstanding behavior patterns and beliefs about our own selves, she and I completed a two-hour exercise that eliminated these patterns at their root source. At last, Stacy managed to remove that "negative voice" permanently, without going back to her old ways. (You can find these exercises through my Confidence at the Core program, which can be linked to from the portal at www.sharonmelnick.com)

Q: In my company, we are going through restructuring and reductions in headcount. How can I prevent myself from getting caught up in the fear and worry about what will happen?

A: This a relevant concern for a lot of people. The balancing act that you want to strike is not allowing the uncertainty to derail your attention, yet at the same time taking actions to keep you feeling secure. Your mantra for how to reduce fear is: *Action replaces fear.* Use the acronym ACTION to remember all that you *can* do, even in the face of uncertainty:

- **Act fully in your current role**—First and foremost, continue your high performance. No matter what happens, it will be important for you to have a record of results. Be so purposeful that the uncertainty in the background is drowned out by your current efforts to concentrate on what's in front of you.
- **Control what you can control**—On the one hand, you're off-setting your fear by giving your all to your current position. On the other hand, you don't want to be in denial about possible eventualities. As always, focus on your 50%. Make a list of all that you can control to reduce the chance of a negative outcome and increase the chance of a positive one. Instead of allowing your thoughts to run wild toward what you can't control, try to pinpoint something *specific* you are worried about in the situation For example: "I'm worried I will lose my job," or "I'm worried that salaries or commissions will be reduced." Then ask yourself, "What can I do right now to have more control over the outcome of this situation?"

    You could make a list of all the people you know in the organization and keep those relationships healthy as well as building new ones at industry conferences and networking events. Reach out to those people, have lunch, share information and, most important, continue to be their resource and support their success.

Are you considering shifting into a new role? Ask them to keep their ears and eyes open for you. Have you assessed whether your worries are based on objective reality or just your self-doubts? Bolster your confidence so you'll trust that you will land on your feet no matter what unfolds.

- **Take steps that hedge against worst-case scenarios**—If you're still worried, buffer yourself against worst-case scenarios: Access your company's trainings on financial counseling or seek out the myriad career development resources available online. Dust off your résumé and get excited about updating it with all you've accomplished since you last edited it. Identify a skill you have that you could teach to others or a long-held dream you never pursued. Then, channel it into that side business you've often thought about but never acted on. It's easier and less expensive than ever. Be more proactive in your networking outside of your organization; you could meet people who are in a position to hire you if your current job doesn't work out (this is a good strategy even if you stay in your current position).[3] Be sure to check out the recommended resources at the end of this chapter.

- **Inform yourself to the extent possible, but don't obsess**—Be proactive about finding information, but don't become so obsessed with learning more that it works to the detriment of your focus. Just be impeccable for your 50%. Remain in "ready position" for whatever information is revealed to you. If you're a leader, be thoughtful about how you convey the information you have to the people around you. In the absence of information, they will default to worst-case scenarios for themselves.

- **Orient your attention away from the current moment**—If you find yourself obsessing over the present moment, you could be caught in the Survival Under Stress cycle. Try shifting your attention away from the moment. Picture yourself in the distant future when you will have more perspective on your life than you do right now. Ask your "future self" what's the best way to proceed in the current situation. Or, use strategies that have helped you in the past to master change (see Chapter 3 for a refresher on realistic optimism). Finally, the simple and easy approach of distraction actually works quite well. I'm not suggesting denial, but rather taking your attention off of fear-inducing subjects, and keeping it on matters that promote a positive state of mind. This simple approach can work wonders!

- **<u>Nip</u> worries in the bud**—We worry as a way of trying to control the future. The irony is that our worrying only occupies the present, which is the one time you have to impact the future. If you know you're a worrier and you don't think you'll be able to break the habit at this point in your life, then turn that trait into a strength: Be strategic with your worries. Use them to think of contingencies that you could help to prevent.

  Try containing your worries by organizing them into "worry hours." In this technique, you quarantine those worried thoughts and set aside a certain amount of time, let's say 15 minutes twice a day. And when I say, "worry," I mean worry hard! Worry until you have resolution so you won't have to worry anymore.

Q: My procrastination is stressing me out. What can I do to stop it?

A: All procrastinators are not alike! Based on thousands of people who have participated in my programs, I've put together a list of the "seven types of procrastinators." If you know what to do but aren't doing it or if you've tried to stop procrastinating but it hasn't worked, it's probably because you haven't found strategies that match your Procrastination Type:

- The Perfectionist
- The Dreamer
- The Avoider
- The Protector
- The Pressure Seeker
- The Prioritizer
- The ADD/Disorganized Type

Dan procrastinated because he was an avoider. He saw the piles as too complex and too time consuming to tackle. That's why he developed a system involving his assistant. He was also a Protector (he protected himself from others' criticisms of his perceived flaws), who didn't follow up on appointments with whale prospects because he thought they were above his level. But Dan grew his business as he learned to Go Direct!

You can take the brief quiz to determine your Procrastination Type and find the right strategies to start taking action at www.sharon melnick.com.

ACTION PLAN

- Listen to an audio training that teaches you how to Be a Better DJ of your Mental iPod by changing negative, critical, doubting or fearful thoughts into ones that are positive and motivated. You can download it for free at www.sharonmelnick.com.
- Fill out your ACCEPT vs. ACCOMPLISH log so you have a game plan how to move past your doubts.
- Start your Intuition Log. Within days you can look objectively at the pattern of successes using your Intuition.
- Identify your Procrastination Type to find the right strategies to start taking action! www.sharonmelnick.com.

POINTS TO REMEMBER

- If you have self-doubts and self-criticism, you can change the source of your stress! The chapter offers five strategies to change the negative, fearful and doubting thoughts that stress you.

- Be a better DJ of your mental iPod. Change the tone of your inner self-talk so that it's self-championing and creates a positive soundtrack to help motivate you.
- Move past doubts by objectively determining your perceived weaknesses and then deciding whether you will ACCEPT vs. ACCOMPLISH.
- Build self-trust through the use of an Intuition Log that helps you track your record of judgments and intuitions, revealing the extent to which you can trust your own intuition.
- Free yourself from perfectionism by identifying the source of your perfectionism, particularly whether it comes from Passion, Prevention of Disapproval, or Prepping for Approval.
- Remember the ACTION acronym to manage your fears about restructuring in your organization.

Recommended Resources

- www.marshallgoldsmithfeedforward.com to learn state of the art feedback approaches.
- www.mygreenlight.com for helpful strategies on how to network effectively for a next position.
- www.brendonburchard.com or www.strategicprofits.com for the blueprint to monetize your knowledge as a business or start a side business.
- www.vervago.com for how to think critically so you can speak up confidently.

SECTION IV

Rx for Relationship Stress

In his play *No Exit*, the existentialist writer Jean-Paul Sartre wrote, *"L'enfer, c'est les autres."* Translation: "Hell is other people." Could it be that Sartre was on the Survival Under Stress cycle? Many of us experience a significant degree of friction in our day-to-day work interactions. More than 75% of the participants in my workplace relationships webinars report wasting 30 to 90 minutes per day (or more) on matters related to interpersonal "friction." Managers can spend up to 42% of their time resolving interpersonal friction.[1] Similarly, www.Monster.com reports that a "bad boss" is the leading cause cited by Americans for leaving jobs. Office stress also invades our home life. When one partner is stressed, the marital satisfaction of both partners sinks.[2]

In my individual meetings with clients, the biggest work challenge people ask me about is not how to run their businesses, but how to deal with *people!* For example, what do you do when you don't get what you need from a direct report or assistant? When your manager is indecisive or unsupportive? When a client is "high maintenance?" When your business partner or family member is stubborn? We've all been there. You try your best to "get the other person to cooperate" and, when they don't, you feel you have no control.

These knocks and frustrations can elicit a stress response characteristic of the Survival Under Stress cycle. What happens then? Negative emotions. Blame. Defensive reactions. We do the "silent scream." Or, maybe we snap at the person. If we say things we regret, we lie sleepless at night, feeling guilty or worrying about the next day's fallout. Some of us do the opposite: withdraw, give the silent treatment, and avoid interacting with the person. Or, we suffer in silence. If we have to interact with that person regularly, a blanket of negative energy or dread may build up within us—and that can be hard to shake off. We're focused only on what *we* need and what we wish the other person would stop (or start) doing. Unable to remain neutral and keep our sights on a constructive outcome, we unwittingly deprive ourselves of the ability to understand (and therefore influence) the other person to make the situation better. When caught in this loop we're distracted from our mission and drained of energy.

There's nowhere more important to practice the 50% rule than in the context of interpersonal relationships. In Section IV, you'll learn to **change your perspective**: keep your thoughts, feelings, and behaviors directed toward progress in your career and life—and not be consumed by friction from that difficult relationship. You'll understand why you act—and more important, *react*—and you'll learn to remove the emotionality that takes you off your game. You will **change your physiology** to remain cool, calm, and collected in the face of relationship stress. You'll learn to **change the problem** so you can influence others and gain their cooperation.

"Take Our Daughters and Sons to Work Day" comes once a year, but every day is "Bring Your Personality to Work Day!" Of course, each of our personalities is different. Dealing with difficult personalities feels like *Mission: Impossible.* "Your mission, if you choose to accept it" is to learn how to work with and through others to accomplish your personal objectives, as well as the mission of the team, client, or organization. No matter how much or how often you encounter resistance from other people, you can always remain on the Success Under Stress cycle.

9

How to Stay Rational When Someone Is Driving You Nuts

"It's impossible to hate anyone whose story you know."
—H.S. BOYLAN

Let's turn on the windshield wipers to get a clear understanding of relationship stress. Clarity isn't only your best time management tool. It's your best conflict management tool as well. It will always be a temptation to sit back, play armchair psychologist, and blame the other person (even though that usually doesn't get you to a resolution). Dealing with *yourself*, however, is the aspect of the situation most in your control—even though it doesn't often feel that way!

When in a tense situation, try sorting out "your stuff" from "their stuff" as soon as you can. Remember, that's the basis of our 50% rule. You may have done more to create or maintain the interaction than you think. Once you change the way you express your 50%, the whole dynamic between you can shift, even radically. But, this is not always true. Why? Because the other person may still be difficult to deal with even after you've been impeccable. Therefore, later in the chapter, you'll find tools to survive (and even thrive) in a variety of difficult relationship scenarios!

When you're on the Survival Under Stress cycle, you're at risk of getting hijacked by emotional responses that cause you to "react."

When you react, your emotional turmoil is disproportionate to the severity of the actual situation. You lose time and focus. You drift away from your Horizon Point. This, in turn, gives you ample fodder for regret. That's the cycle in action!

The best way to keep your relationships supportive of your goals is to stay poised and maintain your presence. To manage yourself toward a constructive outcome, you must think clearly and focus on the facts. Sounds simple, so why is it so hard? To answer this question, you first need to learn how and why you react. Then you can learn approaches to shift from reactive to rational.

Why We React

In some situations, your reaction is minor; in others, you may lose your cool. My definition of a trigger is "a situation that makes you feel powerless or out of control in a way that you have experienced too many times in the past." Here's an example of a trigger and a reaction, courtesy of my client Patricia, a vice president in a merchandising company:

> I was in a meeting with my boss going over the performance reviews of my team. He pointed out where I could have done more to supervise my buyers and, at some point, asked me how I was using my time. I overreacted: I took it personally and got a little testy with him. I thought he was questioning my decisions, which I took to mean that after all these years of working together, I still hadn't proven myself to him. I wondered why he still didn't trust me, and I resented him for it. Once I calmed down and used the method you taught me, I could see that he may have been asking me this because we were onboarding a number of my counterparts and he needed the information as a benchmark to help them manage

their time. If I had responded that way in the moment I wouldn't have had to go back in and apologize.

Why did Patricia react defensively? Because instead of viewing the situation objectively or reading her boss's intention in a bigger context, she fixated on the notion that her boss didn't think well of her capabilities. Based on this misinterpretation, she anticipated an unfavorable review in the future. Notice that Patricia is self-conscious about her competence. In this example, you can see how a trigger is related to the experience of stress. Her boss's opinion of her really mattered to her, but her SNS crewmembers assessed that she didn't have control over her evaluation. Danger! Danger! It's the perfect storm leading to an emotional reaction, not a rational one.

How Not to React: The "Stories" Log

Behind every reaction is a "story." A story is your explanation why an event happened the way it did. Your reaction indicates that something in the experience made you feel powerless and out of control. (Usually this is a repeat pattern for you, even though it's not likely to be evident on the surface.) Let's take another example of a "reaction" and play it in slow motion so you can learn how to control it at each step.

Here's the scenario. Brianna is a solo consultant, who has three children and a husband who also works full time. One morning before work, she is preparing breakfast for the children while her husband is out walking the dog. He calls her from his cell phone: "I can't take Sabreena (their daughter) to school," he says. "Can you?" Brianna reacts, "losing it" on the phone, in front of her kids. As I break Brianna's situation down, think of a recent time when you reacted similarly.

As we go through the five steps to determine how and why you react as you do and what alternative reactions might be better, you will learn how to complete Chart 9.1.

Stories Log				
Column 1 Event	Column 2 Shorthand Story	Column 3 Alternative Stories	Column 4 Horizon Point	Column 5 Response

Chart 9.1

Step 1 Identify the Trigger

The trigger is the fact or event (often something that someone said or did—or something they didn't say or do) that precipitated your reaction. In Brianna's case, her husband's request was the trigger. Identify the event that triggered your situation in Column 1 of Chart 9.1.

Step 2 Identify Your Shorthand Story

The moment she heard her husband's request, Brianna's SNS crewmembers took over. In assessing whether the situation was a threat or not, they had to determine *why* it happened. This explanation or interpretation of the situation is key. If someone in a car behind you honked their horn at you in a parking lot, you'd respond very differently according to whether you thought they were unjustifiably impatient or their child hit the horn playing in the front seat.

Since your stress system needs to respond immediately, it can't gather all the details of the situation. There's no time for a full web search or to philosophize about the underpinnings of human motivation. Those crewmembers need a response pronto! Your brain will use any available shortcuts to save energy and reach a quick conclusion. Brianna's brain simply referenced the current situation in the context of past situations (the brain does an internal search of every experience you've ever had and asks, "How does this makes me think or feel like I did in past threatening situations?"). These shortcuts in your brain tend to be "all-or-nothing" thinking, leading you to jump to conclusions.

To understand why your brain causes you to react, you need to find the source that explains why you felt powerless or out of control. You can use an excavation process to trace the thoughts and feelings associated with the trigger. Start by simply asking yourself the question: "And what does that mean about me?" I call this the "Dig Down." I taught Brianna this process so that she could identify her shorthand story. Brianna's initial automatic story was to explain her husband's call by saying, "He is trying to get out of doing his fair share of household responsibilities. I always have to be the one to do the lion's share of the household chores." Once she had that explanation, she didn't expend any energy analyzing the situation further.

So I asked Brianna that illuminating "Dig Down" question: "And what does it mean about you that he doesn't do as much for the kids as you do?" Her response took us one level down in her shorthand story: "It means that I don't stand up for myself with him." I asked her again: "Ok, so what does it mean about you that you don't stand up for yourself?" This question revealed the next level down of her shorthand story: "It means I end up doing things for other people because I'm not worth other people taking the time to do them for me." I could tell we were on the trail of a file in her memory that was full of emotion for her. So I asked her one more time: "And what does it mean about you that you are not worthy of other people doing things for you?" Her shorthand story at the deepest level was revealed: "I'm not good enough."

When her husband asked her to take her daughter to school, it seemed at first blush that she was angry with *him* for not doing enough to help out. But as we went through the excavation process, she realized that she reacted because his comment triggered her own self-doubt. Though, in fact, her husband asked if she could take Sabreena to school, Brianna's stress system reacted with, "He's asking me to do it because I'm unworthy of having him do it for me!"

When Brianna's thoughts about "I'm not good enough" get activated, she feels bad about herself; she thinks she needs to protect herself from being taken advantage of. That's why she feels deflated and "loses it." When Brianna learned this insight, she was blown away. "I am shocked at why I reacted. But I can see that it's definitely true," she told me. In short, the real reason she snapped was that her husband's question activated her *own* doubt.

In Column 2 of Chart 9.1 (page 164), identify your shorthand story by doing the "Dig Down" process to determine the underlying reason why you interpreted your situation in the way you did. By asking yourself this same train of questions you too can see how your stress response system digs through the archives of your past.

Hopefully now you know a little more about how your brain works and why you react to interpersonal conflicts. At the time, Brianna didn't know how to get past her automatic reaction and onto the Success Under Stress cycle. Feeling hurt and guilty about having "lost it," she started her day off on the wrong foot.

Did you notice that as Brianna reviewed the current situation, she considered only how it affected her? She wasn't concerned with the stresses her husband may have been experiencing that prompted him to make the request or, for that matter, any other contextual factors. In order to prevent a reaction in a broadly similar situation and prevent the cycle of regret, you need to know how to retrain your reactions in the moment.

Step 3 Tell Three Alternative Stories Before You're Allowed to Act

Next, come up with three alternative perspectives on the situation. Tell three different "stories" that explain why the trigger event might have happened. Brianna looked at the context of what had been going on in their lives in the last 24 hours. From that analysis, she developed three alternative stories to explain her husband's request:

1. He was just passed over for a promotion at work and is now convinced that he has to get there on time, or even early. In other words, he was acting out his own anxieties.
2. He was tired because he'd been up late the night before.
3. They hadn't communicated well about what each had on their plate that day. Subsequently, he wasn't aware of all the demands on her that morning and why having to take Sabreena to school would create stress for her.

When you're generating your alternative stories, try to use as much as you actually know about the other person's general tendencies. Write one or two from the other's point of view. Write another from your own point of view where you played a role, but it doesn't mean you're bad or unworthy. For example, "I realize I didn't tell him about my schedule this morning." Any insights you gain from *this* point of view represent an opportunity to improve the situation and prevent it from happening again.

As a general rule, try to train yourself to get to the "benefit-of-the-doubt" story as quickly as possible and consider understandable reasons that might have driven the other person's actions. For example, he may be acting in good faith, trying to accomplish what's important to him even though he went about it ineffectively. This could easily characterize Brianna's husband's request. As you write the stories, consider that the other person could have a longstanding limitation of repeating patterns without being capable of changing them.

Be aware: When other people are acting rigid or unchangeable, it's almost always because they're stuck in their own shorthand story. Unable to look at the situation objectively or tell alternative stories, they see only through the lens of their own stress response and lack empathy for your point of view. It's *very* challenging to deal with someone who feels this way—but at least you can understand why he or she is stuck and not take it personally. You can appreciate that the "stuck" person will remain on the Survival Under Stress cycle. Simply knowing this may enable you to have more compassion and change the tone of your response.

Step 3 is an exercise in being impeccable for your 50%. You think through the facts and the context and respond for the good of all. This comparison reminds us of the difference between when our SNS knee-jerk responds to the first whiff of a threat and when our PNS is brought in to help us think through all the options.

Brianna's subjective shorthand stories were a painful reminder of the past, not a learning opportunity. But her alternative stories pointed her toward constructive communication and problem solving.

Make it a rule to develop three alternative stories before you allow yourself to be upset by a situation (and make it a rule to read emails or texts that upset you two or three times to ensure you understand the other person's intent). Try to learn the skill of defaulting to "benefit-of-the-doubt" stories!

In Column 3 of Chart 9.1 (page 164), write down three alternative stories that help to explain why the other person may have acted the way they did in the trigger situation you identified in Step 1.

Step 4 Choose the Story That Fulfills Your Horizon Point

A key theme of this book is to ensure that your responses are intentional and in the service of your desired outcome. Refer back to the description you came up with in Chapter 3 that encapsulates who you want to be at your Horizon Point. Jot down a few words that remind you of who you want to be in that situation. Brianna's Horizon Point is to be a Powerful, Balanced and Happy person.

Now, select the alternative story—or combination of stories—that will help you be who you want to be at your Horizon Point. Brianna decided on a combination of story #1 (that her husband was anxious about getting to work on time because he'd recently been passed over for a promotion) and story #3 (he wasn't aware of her busy schedule that morning). By reframing the situation, she could *choose* how she wanted to respond. This decision empowered her to feel that she was a powerful contributor to their husband–wife partnership (as opposed to unworthy).

I'm not suggesting that you always have to "think positive" about the other person. The key is that your stories empower you to be at your Horizon Point and communicate respectfully to improve or end the stressful situation. A story that embraces the reality that the other person has limitations and may never be capable of giving you what you need to progress in your work or be happy in life can sometimes be the most empowering story of all. Your stories should give you a more accurate understanding of all the factors at play in the situation, freeing you from emotional reactions that make you feel hurt or angry.

In Column 4 of Chart 9.1 (page 164), write down the phrase that describes who you want to be at your Horizon Point and the story or combination of stories you chose to help you be that person.

Step 5: Take Action in the Service of Your Horizon Point

Steps one through four involved internal preparation. In Step 5, we take action. Initially, the only behavior that Brianna's family saw was Brianna "losing it." Her reaction came from a shorthand story based on the assumption that her husband's request meant she wasn't good enough. But once she viewed the situation from the perspective of her Alternative Stories, she let go of the stressful reminder of feeling unworthy. Constructively and objectively, she decided that at an appropriate time, she'd open a discussion with her husband about "who does what" in terms of household responsibilities going forward. She would also ask him if he wanted to request any morning routine changes in order for him to get to work regularly at an earlier time. That's a pretty different scenario!

In Column 5 of Chart 9.1 (page 164), write the action or response you will take based on your alternative story or stories.

Shorthand stories are common in workplace and family relationships. Most people stop their analysis after they've made their automatic shorthand story in step #2. They think they've accurately explained the other person's behavior (which leaves them frustrated or angry and creates friction where it wouldn't exist otherwise). I've heard countless stories of these automatic assumptions in the workplace. Gary is a client who worked on a business development team at an investment firm and lived on the East coast. One day, his West coast colleague scheduled a meeting with a big prospect at a time Gary couldn't attend. He immediately assumed the colleague was trying to steal credit for the deal. Further examination revealed that the prospect had requested a low-key initial meet-and-greet before pursuing a meeting with the full team of powerhouse investment professionals and that credit would be shared regardless of who was present at the initial meeting.

Erin was a residential realtor in my Confidence at the Core program. When her new assistant didn't show up to cover the apartment Open House as requested, Erin immediately assumed that her assistant was irresponsible or that Erin herself was an incompetent boss. Notice how she labeled herself and her assistant. Shorthand stories! Further examinations of alternative stories revealed that neither boss nor report were incompetent, irresponsible, or unworthy. They'd had a miscommunication. Each had made an assumption. In the end, Erin implemented a better system for communication—a net gain. In my experience, her earlier "black-and-white" thinking and her harsh judgmental voice reflect an early history of difficult or traumatic relationships. These experiences shape a person's stress response pattern into the vicious cycle. That's why it's so important to be proactive about retraining your system to have a Success Under Stress pattern.

The "Stories Log" is a step-by-step approach that takes the emotion out of situations and helps you stay poised to lead in any interpersonal interaction or crisis. The log enables you to see the bigger picture context, give benefit of the doubt, and recognize where your own self-doubts and perceptions of people may be simply retreading well-worn grooves instead of helping you act in the service of your Horizon Point.

You can download the five-column Stories Log at www.sharon melnick.com. With some practice, you'll learn to apply it in real time, ensuring that communications are improved and problems solved more easily (or avoided altogether).

> Q: How can I not react or get defensive when someone criticizes me?
>
> A: You can learn greater resilience to other people's negative feedback by sorting out which aspects of it accurately reflect you and which reflect their own biases. What other people say about you comes through their own filters. People tend to talk to others the way they talk to themselves. If they judge themselves and cut themselves down, they'll judge and cut down others. Conversely, if they accept human flaws and see mistakes as learning opportunities, they'll accept it in others as well.

When people criticize you, they're revealing their own worldview. Determine first whether the person's opinion is trustworthy. Is it objectively about you? Does it have your best interest in mind? If so, be open to their constructive feedback.

> Q: How can I be impeccable for my 50% when dealing with people who are not impeccable for their 50%?
>
> A: It doesn't seem fair. You may even be questioning whether being impeccable for your 50% gives a free pass to others to act badly.

Really, how can you not get caught up in their behavior if it negatively affects you? Good question!

I like to remember that other people have their own psychology and a biology that has motivated their behavior for a long time. We wish we had a remote control button to force them to act the way we want them to, but people will be who they are going to be. We can only control what's within our sphere of control. To stay rational, not reactive, always be impeccable for your 50% and act in the service of *your* Horizon Point.

Interacting with Difficult People

If you have to interact with a difficult person regularly, here are a few strategies to keep you emotionally steady and advancing toward your next-level success.

Clean Up Your Own Backyard

Clean up your own 50% before you complain or blame another person. For example, John, an assistant marketing director at a university participated in my Friction Free Relationships program. He perceived that his boss had a "gotcha!" approach of pointing out his flaws rather than letting him have more say over his function and praising the things he did well. After a while, John was so frustrated at her tone that he was ready to quit. We sorted out "his stuff" from "her stuff." Turns out, "his stuff" was that he was regularly making numerical mistakes on his marketing projections—he wasn't taking ownership of this function. And "her stuff" was that, as a manager, she was critical and micromanaged him.

To play *his* part, John had to be able to operate independently and reliably at his level. Because he found his boss demoralizing, he wasn't motivated to improve his performance for her. So we reframed her behavior into a motivation for him: like a "drill sergeant" giving orders to raise his game for the next role. As a result, he concentrated on developing an internal sense of reward for his accomplishments rather than hoping (only to be disappointed) that she would provide reassurance. (Way to Go Direct, John!) He didn't focus on her behavior or try to change her. Instead, he cleaned up his own behavior and turned obstacle into opportunity. (And, by the way, three months later he was promoted!)

Distinguish Whether It Makes Sense to "Try" or "Stop Trying" in the Relationship

Any ongoing effort with a difficult person is exhausting. You try. They don't change. You blame yourself (and them). You "bang your head against the wall." You're caught in the vicious loop, hoping something will change. Should you keep trying, or stop? Should you stay or go?

When my clients talk about trying to improve interactions, it's usually in the context of trying to change the other person. ("I've tried pointing out her mistakes a million times!" they'll say). That's not effective. Focus on your 50%! Then either you'll see improvement, or you won't—giving you the choice to leave or stay (see also the strategy of Healthy Detachment discussed in Chapter 3).

Usually we make assumptions about what causes the other person's behavior, such as "I'm not important to them." You get angry. Instead, use a decision tree to assess the **WHY** behind their behavior. Is their behavior a **"CAN'T"** or a **"WON'T?"**

Their behavior would qualify as a can't if the person has reached the ceiling of his or her capability, lacks the resources, training, or tools to carry out the project, or if he or she faces a systemic bottleneck that's out of his or her control. Their behavior could be a can't if they're psychologically impaired, or have limited emotional intelligence. In contrast, the person's behavior would qualify as a won't if, for example, they're unmotivated (or have a related attitude issue), if they're acting on knowledge you don't have or if your request is not within the scope of their role.

Think about the difficult person with whom you must interact. Take into account everything you know about that person. Is the behavior a can't or a won't? If it's a can't, is the skill set he or she needs to develop **TRAINABLE** OR **NONTRAINABLE**? If the former, set up the training, coaching, and mentoring. Then, evaluate the outcomes. If your gut says that the person isn't capable of the job even if provided with resources and support, then consider dramatically reducing the scope of their function or begin arrangements for transfer or termination in conjunction with an HR professional. Once you've reached a conclusion, act. Keeping a nontrainable can't person in a role creates friction for the person, for you, and for all the people who are working to produce a result for customers who need your services.

If it turns out the behavior is a won't, you should investigate and problem solve. My client Rosa, for example, a junior partner in a technology consulting firm, wanted the company's subject matter expert to attend an important client meeting with her. For weeks he ignored her request, and she was frustrated! She concluded his behavior was a won't. Now, for the "why." She realized that he isn't compensated for these kinds of meetings, which are really incidental to his objectives. This clarity gave her immediate relief. Subsequently, she asked her boss to make a request of the subject matter expert's boss. As a back up, she inserted his insights into her presentation, so he didn't necessarily need to attend.

In contrast, I coached a senior vice president at a real estate firm. She had a VP direct report who consistently made mistakes in his judgment and didn't meet deadlines. Despite her repeated feedback, his behavior continued. Because she had promoted him, thought highly of his potential, and had a friendship with him, she initially assumed that his behavior was a won't. She tried for months, suffering the toll of sleepless nights. Deeply upset because of all the effort she had put into his development, she took his won't personally—until she had a "light-bulb" moment when she did this exercise. That's when she realized, "Maybe he's overwhelmed by the scope of the job;

maybe he isn't capable" of the level of responsibility. In other words, a can't. She divided his job into two positions and demoted him until he could prove his leadership on key issues. Within two days, she was sleeping through the night, and he soon was performing better.

I've seen many clients make the distinction between can't and won't and literally within one minute transform from frustrated to action oriented! It's always better to face the reality of the situation early on than continuing to beat your head against the wall in the hope that the person will change.

Dan had an undercontributing, difficult business partner, who even got Dan into a suspicious business deal. Through our discussions, Dan realized he was staying in the partnership because he was afraid of a confrontation. Once aware that he was the one blocking dissolution, he was empowered to negotiate an amicable settlement and then felt free to go out and land his deal with the whale clients.

Therefore, what is the correct answer to the question, "Should I stay or should I go?" I say, "Stay" *if it's for the right reasons.* That means you're putting the relationship to the right test by having clarity on what is "my stuff" and "their stuff" and developing a plan for what each person needs to do differently (with accountability built in). If you are *hoping* the other person will change, don't stay. If you're staying only to protect yourself from hurt or because you don't trust yourself once out of the relationship, *go!* Stay only if you're willing to be the only one in the situation who is impeccable for their 50%.

Accept Other People's Levels of Development . . . and Work on Yours!

We've discussed how to determine what actions to take to improve your interactions with a difficult person. In this section, we'll add to our list of "go-to" mantras one that will help you "let go" and stop trying.

Usually when we have to interact with someone who causes us stress, we're inclined to distance ourselves, strike back, or try hard to make it better. But there's a more effective short-term and long-term strategy: unhinge yourself from this automatic inclination. Try to understand the other person and have compassion for them. Stop hoping they will change. Accept that they are who they are.

I hear often from my trainees—who are reasonable, caring people —that they expect the "difficult person" in the interaction to act similar to them. Just because you might take into account other people's feelings or be responsive or supportive doesn't mean that the other person will or that they even have a psychology and biology that is capable of acting similarly. Instead of setting yourself up for disappointment and aggravation at other people's inability to change, you can learn to "accept other people's level of development . . . and work on yours!"

It's helpful to remember that people, generally, do what they do for good reason—even if the reason isn't always apparent to you! Not everyone has evolved to exactly the same level. Some people are more selfish than others; some are narcissists who puff themselves up by putting others down. Their behavior appears to come from arrogance and strength, but actually it comes from feeling powerless and insecure inside. They need other people to validate that they're smart or "right"—all part of a never-ending (and never-fulfilled) quest to build up confidence and overcome the pain of early life experiences and a prewired biology.

You may think, "It's all well and good, but they should keep their issues to themselves and not ruin my life!" And to that, I say: "If that person were capable of Going Direct and being impeccable for their 50%, then they would do it!" The very fact that they have to involve other people reveals their lack of capability. Even taking a few moments to *think* about showing compassion for another person's flaws will go a long way to improving your mood.

Be thankful that you only have to hear their grating voice or negative tone a few hours a day or week at the office rather than every minute of every day (like they themselves must endure on their mental iPods). My advice? Seek out the lessons you can learn from them (however slim) and shift your stance to one of adapting to and protecting yourself from their negative energy.

> Q: How can I deal with someone has a negative energy or is emotionally dramatic?
>
> A: Get a sense of whether the person is capable of change. If his or her behavior is severely inappropriate, repeated, or pervasive (by that I mean not just toward you), you'll conclude that they're not amenable to change. No problem. There's a plan B! Your strategy shifts from hoping the person will change to protecting yourself from that person's negativity. I worked with Ming, who reported to a tyrannical boss at an advertising agency. He arrogantly batted down her ideas; he spoke harshly and constantly changed his mind. Ming used to carry home her frustration and fear—until she developed the strategy of remembering that his flaws were due to his own limitations, not her lack of competence. After that, she didn't try to change him. Even though compassion comes the least naturally when you find someone difficult, thinking kind thoughts and accepting others for their flaws will reduce your stress. As you get onto the Success Under Stress cycle, it's easier to think about the context of a situation and see the interaction from the other person's perspective. This can also help you influence the person, as we'll see in Chapter 11.

Whenever possible, Ming "killed him with kindness," staying on her boss's good side by showing loyalty to him (choosing her battles about when to stick up for her point) and put her requests in terms of how it aligned with his goals or would make him look good. (You may see this as inauthentic and "sucking up," but these strategies are intended to keep the difficult person in a positive emotional state around you, to prevent their rage, and to maximize the ability to get needed responses from them. Rather than an icky feeling of sucking up, empower yourself with this approach. Not only are you protecting yourself, but you're using this person to help you make progress on your good work!)

In Ming's case, these strategies were sufficient to tame her boss's egregious behavior most of the time. And when he did flare, she could detach and protect herself: Ming surrounded herself with an imaginary shield that did not absorb his energy. You could do the same. What metaphor works for you? Go ahead and surround yourself with rays of white light. Place an imaginary glass cone around you. Imagine yourself as a superhero with an iron breastplate that protects you. Be creative. Another tool Ming used (this one's a personal favorite) was to imagine that her boss was speaking in that garbled tone like Charlie Brown's teacher from *Peanuts*. With this approach she respectfully made eye contact as he was speaking, but she didn't internalize the harsh, critical tone. These strategies helped Ming stay engaged and staved off her anger and frustration. She managed to hang on in the job long enough to complete a major client advertising campaign that won them acclaim and set her up as an attractive candidate for a position elsewhere. In short, she accepted her boss's level of development and worked on growing her own skills.

Act Constructively Toward Your Desired Outcome

Like you, I must interact with people who react, blame me, talk off point, or display any number of other behaviors that cause stress. I'll let you in on a little secret: Like many of the trainees in my programs— and maybe like you—my initial, internal response can sometimes be annoyance, blame, or judgment. But I remind myself of the outcome I want, both short term and long term. Usually I want to achieve progress on a specific project, while maintaining a long-term collaboration with my colleagues or clients. So I ask myself: "How can I be at my Horizon Point? How can I lead us toward progress?" Internally, I may be dressing down the other person (in extreme circumstances, I'm using the fancy psychology language I learned in graduate school!). Yet, I will make sure that what I actually communicate through my words, tone, and body language is constructive and in the service of the outcome I want. My subjective, momentary reactions are not important. The only thing that will endure is the material outcome we're there to create. I can facilitate that by doing what's in my power to get the other person back on the Success Under Stress cycle. I keep my tone of voice even. I speak with respect (for example: "Can you help me understand how you approached this?" rather than "You did this wrong!") I insert a neutral "story" so that no one feels blamed ("Sounds like we simply had a misunderstanding. It's all good. Let's move forward.")

Q: How Can I Stop Obsessing About That Difficult Person?

A: In a frustrating interpersonal interaction, you often end up talking to (or about) the offending person in your own self-talk. Likely, it's a variation of, "You shouldn't have acted that way!" or "When you do that it hurts my feelings!" or "When you pull this stuff it creates extra work for me!" And then you cross your fingers and hope that the other person will somehow "get the memo" and stop being so difficult just because you talked to them in your mind. Well, technology has become pretty advanced, but not *that* advanced.

I advise you to shift from rehashing what happened in the past to creating the immediate future you want. Do this by changing the tunes on your mental iPod! Stop talking "to them" or "about them" and instead start talking to yourself. Talk yourself into a better understanding of the situation. Talk to yourself about what you want to feel in the situation, what outcome you want and how you can act to achieve those ends.

Create Positive Relationships

Healthy relationships are an antidote to stress. Cultivate friendships and a network of people with whom you work well and accomplish great things. Dropping your social activities because you have "too much to do" and working all the time is a pitfall. Social support—the feeling that you are cared for and have the assistance of a network of friends and family—is one of the best predictors of happiness at work. Of relevance to the 50% rule, people who *provide* social support are amongst the happiest at work (and are promoted on a faster track too).[1]

Remember back in Chapter 4 when I cited research that found men and women respond to stress differently? Men display a "fight-or-flight" pattern, whereas women display the "tend and befriend" pattern. Under stress, women have higher circulating levels of oxytocin, a hormone that promotes bonding and nurturance. Women are shown to have more positive *and* more negative emotion in response to stress, so it's all the more important to have relationships that counterbalance negative emotion. The bottom line is we all need as much perspective, camaraderie, laughter, and support for our life goals[2] that we can get—and give—in our close relationships with friends and family. If you want Success Under Stress, make it a priority to initiate and nurture close relationships. And, if tension should ever arise, use the tactics covered in this chapter.

ACTION PLAN

- Download your "Stories Log" at www.sharonmelnick.com so you can stop being reactive by learning to do the simple five-step exercise. Practice logging three to five stories in the next two weeks so you can get the hang of it and remember to use the steps "in the heat of the moment." Post what you learned in the forum so others can benefit from your experience as well!

- Think of an example of a stressful relationship with a difficult person. Apply each of the five strategies in this chapter to develop a new understanding and a new approach to the relationship. List immediate actions you can take to reduce the stress and increase the collaboration or amicable communication.

- Take a proactive step to cultivate healthy relationships, show an act of generosity toward others, and make a plan get together with supportive friends and family.

POINTS TO REMEMBER

- When a situation reminds us of times that we felt powerless, it can trigger a reaction.
- Use the five-step Stories Log exercise (Chart 9.1) to help you identify the trigger, identify your shorthand stress story, and tell three alternative stories before you act. Choose the stories that empower you to be at your Horizon Point; and respond in the service of your Horizon Point
- Sort out what's "my stuff" and what's the "other person's stuff" in each situation, and then be impeccable for your 50%.
- Remember to "accept other people's level of development, and work on your own" and protect yourself with shielding strategies.
- To figure out whether you should "stay or go" in a relationship, require yourself to put the relationship to the *right* test by making sure you are effective in your 50% efforts:

  1. Clean up your own backyard.
  2. Determine the reasons behind the other person's behavior (use the Stories Log, can't vs. won't), and identify your blocks to letting go.
  3. Look for opportunities to accept other people's level of development and work on yours.
  4. Determine the constructive outcome you want and act in the service of it.

- Cultivate healthy relationships as an antidote to stress.

Shift Instantly from Anger
to a Cool Head

No matter how emotional your opponents are, you must be calm.
—MARTIN LUTHER KING JR.

We all know that relationship stress can wreak havoc on your emotions. What other kind of day-to-day stress causes us to say things such as, "I wanted to wring his neck" or "I'm ready to blow a fuse?" Because you're responding to another person's behavior that's beyond your control, the wave of emotional reaction can come like a tsunami—with no warning.

Sometimes we're not even aware that a stressful reaction has been induced. Indeed, a recent study found that wives seem to be picking up on their husbands' worries about work. Consequently, they react biologically: the more a husband worries about work when he's home with his family, the more his wife's cortisol levels increase. (And, by the way: No. The opposite effect was not observed!)[1]

When we have intense unpleasant feelings in our body, we need to clear them and get back to a calm state of mind that allows us to make good decisions and be productive. When stressed, physiological patterns that can cause disease linger in our bodies. When we don't know constructive stress responses, many of us turn to unhealthy ones, such as numbing out in front of the television, using alcohol or drugs, or even taking it out on other people. According to neuroscientist Jill Bolte Taylor, author of *My Stroke of Insight*,[2] angry emotions run their course through your body for only 90 seconds. The implication is that if you are angry any longer than that, you are choosing to be. In Chapter 9, we reviewed how to change your perspective so you can understand the other person's actions (and your own) and shift your attitude toward acceptance and compassion. Let's look at a toolbox of techniques you can use to think objectively under relationship fire and recover quickly from stressful emotions.

TOOL #1: *Cooling Breath*

Put this one on your greatest hits list! When you're angry, frustrated, or impatient with someone, it feels as though your body is heating up. We even use metaphors like "my blood was boiling" or "hot under the collar." The antidote is to cool down your physiology, so you can center yourself and respond rationally.

Cooling breath is a reverse breath. You breathe in through your mouth and out through your nose in slow deep breaths. When you inhale through your mouth, open it slightly and breathe in with a sipping motion, as if you were drawing through a straw. Try it a few times now. You should feel a cooling, drying sensation over the top of your tongue. Air that comes in through your mouth is cooler because it's not warmed up by the cilia in your nose.[3]

When people annoy you or are hostile around you, immediately use your cooling breath to avoid reacting. With only a few breaths, notice you stay cool, calm, and collected so you can respond in the service of your Horizon Point and not react in a way you'll regret later.

Bonus: This breath can even calm other people down! Do you remember the story in Chapter 2 about the VP who used to get rattled when around her screamer boss? She'd slip right into her cooling breath to keep herself calm *and* diffuse the "screamer." I have literally stopped fights on the New York City subways from across the car, simply by using my cooling breath!

TOOL #2: *The Massage Chop*

Have you ever gotten a great massage that ends with what I call the "massage chop," in which the therapist rapidly hits the side of his or her hands against your back? You can use this technique to "chop up" the negative energy of anger that may have accumulated around your torso. Put your hands out in front of your chest with your palms facing each other. Make that chopping motion in front of you (run your hands between your throat and your belly)—vigorously—and imagine getting rid of the negative energy. Do it for three minutes. If you're taking it seriously and "chopping" as hard as you can, you'll notice that even after a minute you're practically sweating. And after three minutes you'll feel like you've had a great workout. You'll be recharged before moving onto your next appointment or task.

TOOL #3: *Clearing Breath and Energy Breath*

We all have to deal with toxic people from time to time. The trick is to avoid absorbing their "negative energy." The way to do that is to literally push the other person's energy away and clear it out of your field.

Clearing breath (which yogis call "Breath of Glow") clears and detoxifies your system. By stimulating the diaphragm (located between the heart and the abdomen), it creates a tremendous shift in pressure. This creates an internal massage that helps clear the body of metabolic by-products and absorb nutrients better. Similarly, it can clear away negative thoughts and emotions. The sharp expulsions and rapid pace of Breath of Glow energetically pump the natural fluids around your brain, promoting clarity of thought. It also awakens your emotional intelligence.[4,5]

Energy breath (which yogis call "Breath of Fire") reoxygenates the blood and restores the energy that gets sapped by a difficult interaction.

TOOL #4: *Closing Off Your Energy*

When you have to deal with someone who is negative, try to protect yourself by closing off your energy to them. Cross your arms and cross

TOOL #3a: Clearing Breath

Breath: Breathe out through your nose with a steady rhythm every 2 seconds or so. The force of the exhale should come primarily from your navel area which pushes back towards your spine with each breath out.

Hand Position: Bring together the tips of the thumb and index finger.

Duration: Start doing this exercise for 1 minute and work your way up to doing it for 3 minutes.

TOOL #3b: Energy Breath

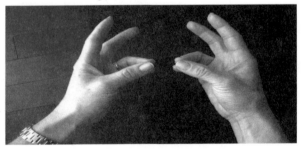

Breath: Inhale and exhale though your nose (in equal proportion) as fast as you can. The force of the inhale and exhale should come primarily from your navel area pushing back towards you spine and then releasing in a relaxed position.

Hand Position: Bring together the tips of the thumb and the tips of the fourth and fifth fingers.

Duration: Start doing this exercise for 30 seconds–1 minute. Work your way up to 3 minutes.

your ankles in their presence. You can also use the hand position in the Clearing Breath (thumb to the fingertip of your index finger), perhaps under the table if you are seated.

TOOL #5: *Emotional Freedom Techniques (EFT)*

Emotional Freedom Techniques (EFT) is a popular clearing/healing method based on the principles of acupuncture. According to master EFT practitioner, Brad Yates, "By tapping with your fingertips on a series of key pressure points, we maneuver the nervous system in a safe and natural way, clearing those uncomfortable feelings that would otherwise stop us from succeeding . . . or even simply feeling good."[6] Doing this tapping technique for just a few minutes can reverse intense feelings of anger, frustration, and guilt. Among a spate of research supporting the efficacy of EFT, a recent study found that tapping dramatically reduces the level of the stress hormone cortisol.[7]

TOOL #6: *Appreciation Breath*

According to the researchers at the Institute of Heartmath, the energy field around your heart is powerfully healing. Indeed, it is 300 times stronger than the one around your head.[8] Put your hands on your heart. Breathe long, slow, and deep while you think about all the people you care about and appreciate. Do this for one to three minutes and you will have shifted into a positive, warm, and glowing energy.

TOOL #7: *Kissing and Hugging*

Here's one of the best all time strategies to get yourself from a state of turmoil to a state of bliss: Kissing and Hugging! We respond to kissing a partner we love by releasing feel-good endorphins.[9] The beneficial effects of hugging and loving touch are immediate and enduring. They ameliorate stress. In one study, 100 couples were engaged in a brief (20-second) hug and 10 minutes of handholding while the other group sat quietly. Then, all of the couples talked for several minutes about an event that made them stressed and angry. Those who had the loving touch before the stressful conversation had greatly reduced harmful physical effects of stress, as evidenced by lower levels of cortisol and increased levels of oxytocin (the nurturing hormone). It appears that loving contact before a tough day at work "could even carry over and protect you throughout the day."[10]

ACTION PLAN

- The next time you notice you are angry or frustrated, use Cooling Breath or the "Massage Chop" to remain calm, cool, and collected.
- Clear your energy with Clearing Breath, and reenergize with Energy Breath.
- Use EFT for more intense or longstanding emotional responses to situations.
- Regularly use the Appreciation Breath to foster states of gratitude and keep yourself happy.
- Be proactive about creating opportunities to counter the harmful effects of stress: kiss, hug, and have loving touch (like hand-holding) with someone you have a loving relationship with. Consider building in a few minutes for this tenderness in the mornings and/or evenings.

POINTS TO REMEMBER

- Stress related to friction in relationships can cause immediate and enduring changes in your physiology. You have more control than you think to clear these negative emotional states.

- The following tools were introduced for use on an as-needed basis to clear your energy after getting emotional about relationship stress. They are all great to use as "recovery" activities during your Sprint-Recovery pattern approach to your day:

    - Cooling Breath and the Massage Chop can be used to dissolve anger.
    - Clearing Breath followed by Energy Breath and Emotional Freedom Techniques can be used to clear a build up of emotions in the body and then reenergize the body toward positive energy states.
    - Appreciation Breath can be used at anytime to experience gratitude and a quick shift into a positive emotional state.

Recommended Resources

- See www.sharonmelnick.com for demonstrations of the tools in this chapter.
- EFT Resources: www.eftvideos.org
- www.Heartmath.org to learn more about the stress-transforming effects of heart intelligence and how to access states of compassion.

How to Get Other People
to Stop Stressing You Out

"Motivation is the art of getting people to do what you want them
to do because they want to do it."
—DWIGHT D. EISENHOWER

If you're a manager, you get things done by influencing people to
do their part. If you're a business owner, you influence prospects or
customers to believe that you have the right solution to their problem. If you start a venture, you need to influence people to back your
ideas. With all that in mind, it's easy to see why failed influence creates stress.

When you can't get other people to do what you expect of them,
your progress gets blocked. You feel as if you aren't being heard. As a
result, you become angry and may assume the other person is disre-
specting you. Before you know it, you're on the Survival Under Stress
cycle, fixated on someone else's lack of cooperation. In this state, you
may forget that you'll be most successful influencing other people
when you're actually trying to understand or help them rather than
just looking out for your own interest.

Influencing someone means moving that person toward taking
action willingly. Remember, most people these days are doing their
best, but are overwhelmed. They barely have time to read or listen, let

alone remember what they read or heard. Their own priorities—not yours—are at the tops of their minds. Under stress, they default to their reactive patterns. The New Normal creates conditions ripe for misunderstandings and crossed communications. Now that you've ingrained the philosophy of Be Impeccable for Your 50%, you may ask, "How can I get someone else to change their behavior if I can only control my 50%?"

Each person arrives at an interaction with you bearing a unique history of work and life experience that has shaped them. They filter the interaction through their fears, frustrations, and strong motivations. They have a distinct personality and communication style. He may not share your values, your assumptions, or your desired outcomes. If you want to influence him, it's up to you to understand what levers to pull, and it's up to you to bridge the gap in your personality or communication style. That's what it means to be impeccable for your 50%.

Four Principles for Influencing Others

When interacting with other people, especially in situations where there's resistance to following your direction:

- Influence for *their* reasons, not for yours.
- Customize your communications to cut through resistance.
- Transfer ownership of the problem.
- Lead with generosity to create a bigger game.

Influence for Their Reasons, Not For Yours

Think about a situation in which you want to influence someone. You might begin by listing all the reasons you think your proposed course of action is a good one. And then you'd explain them to the person you want to influence. The problem is that you're assuming other people will change or take action just because you're convinced it's the right thing to do.

During my early years of graduate school, I spent a few summers working with children who were diagnosed with a syndrome called "Oppositional Defiant Disorder." That essentially means they show a consistent behavior pattern in which they argue, talk back, disobey, and defy parents, teachers, and other adult authority figures. Imagine trying to tell a child with these kinds of tendencies to stay in line or clean up after himself! I learned that I could never ask them to do something just because it was important to me or because it was the rule. I could only strengthen my leverage with them if I aligned my request with what *they* wanted.

The cardinal rule of influencing other people is to frame your requests in terms of What's In It For Them (WIIFT). Everyone is motivated for his or her own reasons. Their reasons for taking action are not the same as your reasons for wanting them to take action. For strong leverage, figure out WIIFT!

People are motivated on two levels. The first is defined by their business function. We're always motivated to achieve the bottom line in our work because that's what we're being paid to do. Plus, it's what we're good at. Examples of appealing to a *business* WIIFT include: They want to complete a project; make decisions faster or meet deadlines; make or save more money; get promoted or have more responsibility; have more time; ensure a successful event; stay in their job or advance in their career; enjoy a more flexible working schedule. You always want to figure out how to align what you're asking them to do with how it's going to be in the service of their business bottom line.

Second, we're motivated on a *personal* level—and personal motivation can be more powerful than business motivation. Observe the person, listen to what she says, and ask questions to discern her personal WIIFT. The more specific and the more emotionally salient you can articulate the WIIFT, the easier and more powerful the influence you will have. Examples include:

- They want to be recognized, approved of, awarded, respected, or thought of as "the hero."
- They are conflict avoidant and just want to hold onto their job and not make a mistake.
- They want to get things done; they are results driven.
- They want to be creative and engage in self-expression.

Whatever you have determined to be the other person's WIIFT, simply frame your request in terms of how doing your task will help her achieve what she wants. Why swim against the current? Attach your request to an already running stream of her own preexisting motivation, and it will be easy for her to say yes.

Examples of This Powerful Approach

An attendee at a training program at a media company followed up with me. Elizabeth was responsible for internal advertising. She was concerned about an event that had occurred with one of her internal clients that resulted in friction between the departments and a slow-down in work. She approached her boss, the head of the division, three times, requesting a resolution of the issue. Elizabeth explained that her department's numbers were down and something needed to be done. And, each time, Elizabeth left the meeting empty handed. Her boss never honored her request. She felt thwarted and stressed—until we identified the boss's WIIFT. A conflict-avoidant person, Elizabeth's boss was people oriented; she always sought to maintain harmony. So Elizabeth approached her boss again, this time pleading her case by taking the boss's WIIFT into account: "People are experiencing bad blood, the communication is down, and my team members are upset about it."

What do you think happened? Of course, within five minutes the boss called her counterpart in the other department and dealt with the issue. Why? Because Elizabeth made her request in terms of what was important to her boss, not to her. Sell for *their* reasons, not yours!

At a workshop on influence at a bank going through a lot of changes, a talented insurance broker asked me how to deal with an older employee—a company veteran who was the point person on operations. She had to go through him to get any resources she needed. But, he never got back to her, he assigned her undertrained support people, and he was, as she put it, "all about him." So she applied what she learned and during the next interaction, she appealed to the personal level of his WIIFT. Though initially she was resistant—loathing the idea of being so kind to someone for whom she had negative feelings—she tried finding the aspects of his role she could genuinely appreciate: "You could really be helpful on this," she told him. "Thank you for the help you have been providing. You've been key to helping us win these assignments." The result? The next week I got a call from her saying, "It was a 180-degree difference. I got all four approvals I needed from him this week!"

Any time we want someone to purchase our services or products, we should be thinking about the WIIFT. We can get so enamored with our offering's features and benefits that we forget to "get out of our own mind" and into the mind of the buyer. When you do this effectively, it can help you to command greater fees and accelerate the buying process. For example, Terrin, an educational consultant and coach, works with principals of failing schools (and do we ever need her to be successful!). In my coaching group for business owners, she revealed she wasn't having enough conversations with principals that led to engagements. And, she said, she felt frustrated: too shy to raise her fees, she was unhappy that she undervalued her own services.

Terrin began engaging principals in conversations that emphasized their business WIIFT. For example, they could reduce tension in meetings with teachers, graduate a higher percentage of students, and free up more time to work on grants. She also appealed to the principals' personal WIIFTs by telling them they'd be respected in their communities. As the principals began to see that they could reduce stress *and* leave a legacy, they grew eager to engage Terrin.

Now, think of a time when you wanted to influence somebody but couldn't. Take the next three minutes and try to identify their WIIFT, both at the business and personal levels. Then phrase your request in terms of their WIIFT. The WIIFT approach is a concept you can use everywhere in your life. Take a fun example. If you're a parent, you might not want to tell your child to get into the car to go to the dentist. Instead you'd say something like, "Let's go visit the lady who puts those fun toys in your mouth and then gives you a (sugar-free) lollipop!!" Use the WIIFT every time. It works!

What is the situation?

_____

_____

_____

What is the person's business WIIFT?

_____

_____

_____

What is their personal WIIFT?

_____

_____

_____

Customize Your Communications to Cut Through Resistance

Often, we interact with people who have a different style or mindset than our own. You may perceive other people as "difficult" to move to action, when in fact they are simply motivated differently than you

—or at least in different ways from those you've been using to influence them. Let's talk about how to bridge differences and remove resistance from the influencing process.

A classic scenario that creates friction in our work lives is when our communication style doesn't match the other person's. For example (this is a generalization based in research), men and women often communicate in different styles. Whereas men are wired to speak in "headlines," women are wired for "stories."[1] Another way of categorizing people is according to their "personality" style. You're probably familiar with the Myers–Briggs assessment distinguishing introverts from extroverts.[2] Some people are more oriented toward visual cues, while others are primarily auditory or kinesthetic.[3] Now that we live and work in a global economy, we're constantly interacting with people from other cultures who have very different points of view and who may interpret information differently than we do.

When it comes to influencing people, a helpful tool is the assessment of social style—yours as well as other people's.[4] People exhibit four distinct social style behavioral patterns, each with its own likes and dislikes. Being aware of each style is critical to understanding the other person's perspective and your ability to adapt your style or approach to solve problems.

Driving Style—Action-oriented people who focus on results and outcomes rather than relationships. They are valuable because they help drive progress, but they can be seen as impersonal and domineering. When trying to influence a driver, be direct and clear; get to the point quickly. Provide useful facts and information. Come to them with convictions. And, if you have questions, ask "what" and "when." Give them an outcome to achieve through their own route rather than tell them exactly what to do.

Expressive Style—Creative, warm, and spontaneous people who appreciate personal recognition. Expressive people are casual. They make decisions based on their instincts and they might not be perceived as being good with details. Make a personal connection with them and share lots of information. Inspirational stories and clear pictures motivate them. Because they're prone to follow the opinions of people they consider important, it's a good tactic to include the opinions of other influencers in your pitch to them.

Amiable Style—Relationship-oriented people who focus on personal interactions, trust, and personal comfort. They are the glue that holds teams together and forges relationships across departments. But they can be perceived as slow workers because they make time for socializing and seeking consensus. Approach them with friendly discussion, and influence them with understanding and mutual respect rather than positional power. Spend time with them so they can air their concerns and apprehensions. And be responsive to these objections. Try to reduce their sense of risk taking by assuring them that you will stand behind them if they support you.

Analytical Style—Information-focused, logical people who consider thinking and analysis critical. Because they want to make sure the task is done right, they can be seen as reserved and slow moving. When trying to influence an analytical person, it's most effective to demonstrate proof. Make information available to them. Step them through your reasoning to arrive at the recommended solution. Be responsive to their questions and patient with their deliberative process. They need to know that supporting you will not lead to a mistake.

Not only can you customize your language and social style, but you can also choose the type of influencing strategy that matches your audience's interests. Most of us default to an influencing strategy that uses numbers and data to convince others. This approach works well in data driven companies, with drivers, and with "left-brain" types, such as engineers, scientists, and accountants. But remember: building a business case isn't the only path to persuasion. You should expand your arsenal of effective influencing approaches. Some situations call for a more inspirational or emotional appeal, one that takes people outside of their day-to-day tasks and connects them to a higher sense of purpose or hope for a better future. Many political campaigners use this strategy.

Example of This Powerful Approach

Consider the example of Raj, who attended one of my training seminars on Influence. He was having trouble getting through to a peer who was rigid about defending her own agenda. At the seminar, Raj learned about building a coalition and appealing to an opinion leader that he knew his peer respected. Subsequently, the opinion leader spoke to the peer on Raj's behalf. That was more convincing than a presentation of his best pro and con arguments.

Transfer Ownership of the Problem

Let's now turn our attention to situations in which you have unsuccessfully tried to influence the other person's behavior. Call to mind a person you interact with who fits one of these criteria. They are:

- Unresponsive.
- Showing an inappropriate or unproductive attitude.
- Unwilling to change their behavior.

When the person you're thinking of displays these traits, whose problem is it? That's not a trick question! Your first thought may have been, "It's their behavior, so it's their problem." True, it may ultimately be the other person's problem, but let me rephrase the question: Who feels the brunt and the frustration from that person's behavior right now? That's right, it's you! And that means it's *your* problem.

As long as the problem is primarily yours, not theirs, the other person will have little motivation to do anything about it. The key is to get the other person to experience his own behavior as a problem. To accomplish that you must **transfer the ownership of the problem**.

To get the other person to share ownership of the problem, use the F-I-R-E technique (**F**act, **I**mplication, **R**espect, **E**xpectation), a step-by-step template for a dialogue to change the problematic behavior. Because you're now accustomed to Being Impeccable for Your 50%, you know you must approach the conversation with the intention to work toward a mutually beneficial resolution.

Begin the conversation with a neutral opening so you won't put the other person on the defensive. For example, Kathy, who participated in my Multicultural Women's Development program, manages a sales team at a technology company. She had a salesperson on her team who was logging too much personal time and had a negative attitude in meetings.

Kathy's first step was to look at the salesperson's WIIFT so she could appropriately and respectfully frame the request for the person to change her behavior. Kathy discerned that the woman wanted to advance and, because she was a single mom, she wanted more money. Once Kathy had a good idea of the salesperson's WIIFT she was ready for the rest of the conversation.

F-I-R-E Technique

Facts: Introduce the behavior you need the person to change. State the facts; only refer to behaviors that are documented, specific, and observable so that both you and the person can evaluate when/if the behaviors change. For example, instead of saying, "When you pull an attitude," Kathy could say, "When you speak in a tone that is critical of the direction the group is going, it sounds more like a complaint than a constructive solution. . . ." Or, "When there are three hours per day logged as personal time. . . ."

Impact or Implication: The next step is to state the implications of their behavior: ". . . what happens is . . ." and then describe the downstream effects of the documented, specific, and observable behavior you just described. You'll be tempted to describe the implications that occur for *you*. It's fine for you to make the person aware of their effect on you, but based on what we've been discussing, you now know that people are more likely to be motivated to change behavior when it impacts the achievement of their WIIFT. Connect the dots between their behavior and the way it's interfering with their business and/or personal WIIFT. "What happens is, your comments carry a tone that makes others uncomfortable and results in them not seeing you as a senior person on the team." Or, "What we look for when we want people to advance in the organization is integrity. We look for someone who contributes a positive tone and works toward group resolution rather than addresses personal issues in a negative tone. . . . And the reason for that is. . . ." This made it clear to the salesperson that if she continued her current behavior it would impede her advancement.

Respect: The "R" stands for respect. Approach people with respect by giving the benefit of the doubt and contextualizing possible constraints that cause their behavior. For example, Kathy could say, "I respect that you are under a lot of pressure and may be frustrated with current sales efforts." Or, she could have added: "I can appreciate you were frustrated in the situation and felt an urgency to raise the matter in our staff meeting . . . ."

Expectation (or request): In this step, you set an expectation or make a request so that the person is clear about the behavior you want to see going forward. For example: "I request that if you have disagreements, bring your concerns to me directly so we can problem solve without introducing a tone that creates conflict on the team." Or, "Here is the expectation that I have of people who want to be on this team. . . ." Or, "Here is what we expect of people who want to be considered as candidates for promotion. . . ." Depending on the situation, you may be in a position to indicate a consequence—"I want to be clear that I will need to see XYZ behaviors in order for you to continue being a part of the team."

Transfer the Ownership

Drum roll please . . . By now you've set the stage. In the previous parts of the conversation, you identified the behavior, described how it's interfering, and stated what you expect of the other person. Now it's time to transfer the ownership—neutrally, genuinely, and respectfully. You even want to say what comes next with concern and support in your voice, because you're invested in helping them achieve their WIIFT: "So, what is **your** plan for how to accomplish this?"

It will be natural for you to want to step in and make a plan for the other person, suggesting what they do and how they should make a timeline to complete it. But if you do that, you'll be maintaining ownership of the problem. That's not good for the other person's development, and it won't alleviate your frustration. Instead, do what comes *un*naturally to you: allow a moment of silence during which the other person can step forward and take responsibility for the problem. Imagine you've duct taped your mouth. Sit on your hands. Do whatever it takes, but wait for them to talk! Let the silence work for you.

So far in this conversation you've established how it's in their interest to do what you're asking of them. Now the issue is no longer between "you and them," but rather between the part of them that's responsible for the behavior and the part that's motivated to achieve their WIIFT. You shift the power dynamic and move yourself into a support role. It's appropriate for you to ask: "How can I support you in your plan?" Or, "What do you need from me?" You also want to establish an accountability plan. You may want to ask: "What do you think would be helpful to keep accountable to the plan that you just made?" Or, "Let's make a plan to check in with each other and see how you're progressing."

This exercise builds tremendous awareness for you too. It can reveal your own tendency to take on the responsibility for other people's behavior. Being too responsible for others is stepping over your 50% and into theirs. It brings you stress, and it deprives the other person of an opportunity either to develop needed skills or to find another role that's a better fit and will lead to greater personal mastery.

Example of This Powerful Approach

Stacy used this very method with her underperforming direct report. Gaining clarity on his inability to improve performance was a key factor in moving him out of her group and subsequently freeing herself from being "in the weeds." Her F-I-R-E conversation sounded like this:

*Fact: "When we have reviewed the contracts together over the past two months, we've uncovered several instances in which you did not identify key risk-related clauses and haven't used language with clients that has been vetted. . . ."

*Implication: "What happens is, I have to stay involved in overseeing your work at a detailed level—and that takes up a lot of my time. I'm sure it makes you feel scrutinized, as though you don't have the autonomy to do your work. Those mistakes are keeping me from trusting you to remain the point person with clients. . . ."

*Respect: "I appreciate that some of the work is new to you and that the volume of contracts can be overwhelming. I understand that we can't catch every detail."

*Expectation: "Given the sensitivity of the contracts we are reviewing and the scrutiny our company is under by government regulatory agencies, I need to rely on someone in your position to use judgment before sending out documents to clients. I am going to ask you, for the next 30 days, to run each contract by me after you edit it. In order for you to remain on this team, I need you to show that you're following through on the language we have discussed. . . . Here is what I will be looking for. . . ." Stacy followed up by building a plan to check in.

Notice that in this approach her tone is neutral and respectful— yet firm. Another helpful by-product of this conversation: it yields clarity. Once you have this conversation, there's no question about whether or not they're aware of their behavior. You get your answer as to whether their behavior is a CAN'T or a WON'T, and your path forward becomes clear. In Stacy's case, her direct report was unable to fulfill the criteria she set forth; it became clear he was not the right person for the role.

Allow this conversation template to give you the structure for approaching someone whose behavior is interfering with forward progress (not to mention causing you personal aggravation). Now that you have scripts of exactly what to say, there's no excuse for putting off the conversation!

Take three minutes to script out each line of the conversation. Now you're ready to schedule the meeting with the person. Can you feel the relief of transferring ownership of that problem?

Fact

Implication

Respect

Expectation

Q: How can I influence someone who is upset?

A: When someone is upset they're not in a state that's receptive to your influence. Keep in mind this phrase: "Match Before Move." That means the other person needs to know that you match how they feel before they will move toward your influencing outcome. For example, I coached a woman who was the head of a call center. Her employees received a flat bonus, and she was concerned morale would be low and productivity down. We discussed how she could "Match, Before Move." Her first step was to gain credibility with the employees by empathizing with their disappointment and anger. "I imagine you might be disappointed with our bonus packages. . . ." Once they knew that she understood where they're coming from, she began to move them. "Let me put these numbers in context for you," she explained. "We closed three call centers, but we were able to keep this one open and maintain our salaries. Here's what we have in place to improve our numbers going forward. . . ."

Lead with Generosity to Create a Bigger Game

In business settings where people are often distracted and pressured for time, the best way to get someone's attention is to lead with generosity and authenticity. This is the relationship building approach taught by Keith Ferrazzi, CEO of Ferrazzi Greenlight, author of *Never Eat Alone: And Other Secrets to Success, One Relationship at a Time*, and eminent expert in professional relationship development: "The more generous you are in offering your humanity, and then your knowledge, advice and talents, the more willing other people will be to share themselves with you."[5] The more you take an interest in helping other people, the more you will be seen as a resource. Soon you'll be leapfrogging resistance and gaining cooperation. Creating goodwill is a way of transcending friction. Or, in the words of Dale Carnegie, "You can be more successful in two months by becoming really interested in other people's success than you can in two years by trying to get other people interested in your own success."[6]

Use this approach to grow your network. The more people you can call on to help you get things done, the faster you'll achieve your next level of success—and the more opportunities you'll have for the social support that counteracts stress. I often hear from overwhelmed businesspeople that they don't have time for networking. So I turned to Ferrazzi for advice. He notes that once businesspeople develop the mindset that networking is a priority, they make time for it. He maintains: "Networking is a part of your job because people are a critical success factor of your job." He reminds us that a map of WHO is important to spend time with in order to learn and grow your success is just as important as your list of WHAT actions to take, and offers the idea of a Relationship Action Plan to guide your deepening of strategic, operational and personal relationships.[5] At the end of this chapter, you'll find recommended resources for growing your social network.

Example of this Powerful Approach

Here's an authentic approach (with stunning results) practiced by Louise Guido, CEO of the Foundation for Social Change (her story about funding the Foundation by turning its content into paid mobile applications was discussed in Chapter 3). Guido started the Foundation with no contacts, no funding, and a vague mission. Now, she is on the world stage demonstrating deep strategic partnerships with the United Nations, telephone handset manufacturer Nokia, business software giant SAP, and numerous other corporations and other nongovernmental organizations. She consistently used three approaches:[7]

- "Lead with what the other person wants, what they would see as a unique reason for working with you (don't be the norm like everyone else.) When I walk into a meeting, I've done my homework and I know what appeals to them and can fill a need."
- "Present an opportunity. . . . I will always invite them to an event we're doing or introduce them to someone who could be helpful to their business. Even if the very first meeting yields no tangible outcome, we've started a dialogue. Not everyone is a believer in what you do in the beginning. You have to make them become a

believer in you by constantly engaging them. Tell people what you are doing, have them participate, make them a strategic partner. Too often people want instant gratification, instead of building relationships. For example, we wanted to establish ourselves as important but didn't want to take five years to do so. We came up with an awards program that enabled role model corporations to tell their stories and network with one other. When we first gave that award I would have loved to do business with all of those companies, but we couldn't have gone to them asking, 'We are a new organization, can you give us money?' The conference opened the conversation for us, and now we are doing business with the recipient corporations for whom it makes good business sense."

- Start by using credibility based on your affiliations. Use someone else's name that you work with. Guido says: "If you are working with client A and you want to see client B, they will see you because you are working with client A. . . . I began my partnership with the United Nations because I had the *Wall Street Journal* as the sponsor of one of my prior events. You have to find the hook —another organization or company that is better known than you, that's how you get in the door. You have to build a relationship in which they have the perception that they are going to get more out of it than they give."

I asked Guido how to take this approach when you already have a lot on your plate. Her response: "If you have a lot to do and you are overwhelmed, you have to be discerning: trust your judgment to make sure the other person is genuine. Some people are takers—if it doesn't work out, you move on. Just get out of your own head, and have the attitude: 'let me help somebody.'"

ACTION PLAN

- Think of a situation in which you want to influence someone who has been resistant. Go through each of the exercises in the chapter to build your Influencing Strategy. Identify their WIIFT (What's In It For Them) at the business and personal levels and then frame your request in terms of WIIFT. Identify the person's communication and social style, and then make sure the approach you use with them aligns with the style that gets the best out of them. Consider the type of influencing strategy that will have the most impact on them. Script your approach before you go into the meeting so your communication is intentional.
- If you have to deal with someone's behavior that has aggravated you for a long time, use the F-I-R-E (**F**acts, **I**mplication, **R**espect, **E**xpectation) technique. Spend some time scripting out each of the lines before you have the conversation. Remember to maintain a neutral and respectful tone. After all, with this conversation you're gaining clarity and transferring ownership of that problem!
- Networking to grow influence is a key part of your success, even when you have too much to do. Create your Relationship Action Plan of WHO you need to have relationships with in order to have the next level of success you want.

POINTS TO REMEMBER

- Always identify the intrinsic business and personal motivations of the person you want to influence. Frame your request in terms of how doing your task will help them achieve what they want. It's always easier to enter into a moving stream than to swim against the current.

- To reduce resistance to your message, customize your communications to the style of your listener. There are four social styles: driven, expressive, amiable, and analytical.
- When someone is not changing their behavior despite your wish that they would, it signals that their behavior is a problem to you, and not to them. Incentivize them to change their behavior by transferring ownership of the problem to them. Do that using the F-I-R-E technique conversation template (Facts, Implication, Respect, Expectation) and build accountability into the plan.
- Goodwill can transcend friction. Lead with generosity and authenticity to create strong relationships. Grow your network to help you get things done faster by always having some way you can give to, help, or extend an invite to the other party.

Recommended Resources

- www.sharonmelnick.com for video demonstrations of the influencing strategies and scripts.
- www.mygreenlight.com for resources from Keith Ferrazzi's organization on how to grow the quality and quantity of your network with generosity and authenticity. It also includes information on your Relationship Action Plan
- www.tracomcorp.com for information on Social Styles.

SECTION V

Create Success Under Stress All Around You

Being "impeccable for your 50%" is an approach you can apply in all aspects of your work and personal life. In Chapter 12, I'll give you strategies for leveraging your 50% control toward attaining a work–life balance.

As you begin to experience Success Under Stress, others will notice your calm, confidence, and productivity. You will automatically become a role model. You will be empowered to create conditions that help not only you, but help other people take charge of their stressful circumstances as well. Be proactive and start looking out for these opportunities. In Chapter 13, I'll give you ideas for creating a family, team, and community in which clarity is the norm, reactivity and conflict are reduced, and ideal results are created—all because each person follows the 50% rule.

12

A New Perspective on Balancing Your Work and Life

Work–life balance: that elusive pursuit. When people think about stress, work–life balance is often the first challenge to come to mind. *"How can I be present and give my best at work and be present and give my best at home?"* And it is the number one wish children have for their parents: to come home less stressed and tired. The debate that has lit up the community forums has been whether we can "have it all" or not.[1] One aim of this book is to expand your definition of work–life balance beyond the number of hours you spend at and away from the office.

Every strategy discussed in *Success Under Stress* is relevant to your quality of life. As you have more balance in your day (e.g., sprint-recovery pattern, minimize interruptions, "connect-the-dots time") you'll experience a greater "balance" outside of work—more time and space to think, less reactivity, and more positivity. Using the physiology techniques to clear away the build up of stresses throughout the day avoids the accumulation of stress into exhaustion by the end of the day or week. The Success Under Stress cycle fuels you to have wins, overcome obstacles, and substitute self-confidence for self-criticism, thus giving you more freedom. Being impeccable for your 50% and telling stories in the service of your Horizon Point prevents the wear and tear that interferes with your quality of life. The net effect: a better quality and quantity of energy during your long days as well as your evenings and weekends.[2]

Jason Rubinstein, a vice president at video rental giant Redbox elegantly summarizes the three challenges of successful working people, especially parents: "First, the balance of having a career that is rewarding but still fulfills my role at home as a provider. Second, is time management: What time do I have to leave work and what time am I getting home, how much quality time will I get with my kids every day. The third is how to manage in our 24-7 networked world. The reality is for all the professionals I know, we are doing the best we can and it's hard as hell."[3]

In addition to all the strategies provided in this book, here are some ideas to achieve a work–life balance.

Change Your Perspective

What people really want (and need) is not work–life balance, but to live deeply satisfying lives both personally and professionally, according to Matthew Kelley, author of *Off Balance: Going Beyond the Work Life Balance Myth to Personal and Professional Satisfaction.*[4] Orient your life around having more satisfaction rather than counting the hours at work or outside of work. Part of doing your 50% is coming up with a clear definition of what career success and personal happiness is for *you.* Take some time to write out a vision of what dissatisfies you currently and what you really want in your life. (Revisit some of the exercises in Chapters 3 and 5 to help you.) Then put in place a step-by-step game plan to get on the path toward that deeply satisfying life.

Carol Evans, the dynamic founder and President of Working Mother Media, offers perspective on the guilt many of us face when our work lives and personal lives are out of balance.

What we found in our research is that it's helpful to switch from your everyday perspective to the big picture and stay focused on the long range goal: When you remember, 'I am working to earn money so I can live in this neighborhood that I like and send my children to good schools,' it takes the guilt away. Our research also shows that when a woman thinks about her job as part of a career rather than 'just a paycheck,' she is much more likely to feel satisfied and positive in all aspects of her life.[5]

In her interview, Evans pointed out the importance of outside support:

Having a third party perspective to think through your choices with you is invaluable. . . . That's the reason I get so much out of executive coaching. I feel like a big load of stress and guilt is lifted off my shoulders as I go through that 'aha' moment when my coach reminds me who I am as an individual. For example, when I feel I have been running around the country too much and not paying enough attention to my kids, I have to be reminded: I'm a high activity person at home, too. When I'm home, I'm all out for my kids, challenging myself with them, creating great experiences with them, focusing on them, just like I am at work. How can I feel guilty about that? It's who I am!

Other pioneering women who have been successful at managing a highly accomplished career while raising a close-knit family echo these sentiments. One such pioneer, Andrea Hansen, President of the Bochic Group, reflects:

Becoming a mother teaches you not to judge other people —things that work for other people won't necessarily work for you. Early on I was my worst critic in so many ways—that paranoia that because I'm a working mother my kids will get less love and less time with me. But I know for a fact I am a better mother because of the accomplishments and the self confidence I've gotten from my career.[6]

Change the Problem

Integrate Your Worlds

Keith Ferrazzi, CEO of Ferrazzi Greenlight business relationship experts, advises "blending"—integrating your two worlds—so you're not constantly faced with choosing one over the other.[7] Though some people have justifiable constraints to this, ideally he encourages us to have close, personal and authentic relationships with people in the work place. Keith typifies highly successful individuals with jam-packed schedules and shared his personal approach to *blending*: "We all have to make choices, something will have to give. In our case, loose social ties have given. To keep any social ties we have to blend them: either you join me and my kid for a workout, or I invite you to a dinner with my clients and associates."

Reach for the Flex

According to Carol Evans, "a flexible work arrangement (or creating a schedule of your choice if you are in business for yourself) is the most compelling solution right now for improving the stress of balancing work and life commitments." How can you get started on making a flexible arrangement for yourself? Evans advises:

> First, find out what your company's flex policies are, . . . Be direct and ask the proper authority, your manager or HR professional. Many companies have put flexible work arrangement in place; they are there for the taking. . . . Look around and see what flex arrangements people are actually using—whether formal or informal, or you can take a leader-

ship role and try a flexible work arrangement that works for you.[8]

Evans encourages all of us to see that increasingly "Flex" is no longer just a working mother's issue. More and more younger employees are asking for flexible arrangements. She offered an example from her own company: "There is guy here who runs marathons and he uses flex to practice for his big events. There is no difference between him and a mom who wants leave at 4PM to be with her third grader who is struggling in school. Make sure you ask for what you want. Have a plan. Be prepared to get a 'no' as a first answer."

But, she encourages: "Don't ever give up. Organizations can evolve as well. Many companies that weren't offering flex are now offering it because they found that flexibility increases employee satisfaction and lifts morale."[9] Studies show flexible schedules improve employee health, reduce emotional exhaustion, psychological distress, and work–family conflict.[10,11] Up to one-third of employees are even willing to change employers for such flexible working arrangements.[12] Some companies have found that when applied on a large scale, flexible work arrangements can save an average of 35% on real estate.[13]

Reduce Guilt by Sharing Responsibilities

What do women feel more judged about than not spending enough time with their kids? The messiness of their homes, according to research by Working Mother Research Institute.[14] Sixty-eight percent of working moms in a recent national study feel significantly or strongly guilty about their not-clean-enough homes. Says Evans: "One set of solutions doesn't come from the workplace—our brightest hope now is to work toward a sense of shared responsibility at home."[15] As mentioned in Chapter 5, recent research indicates that men are doing more household tasks. But, according to Evans, we are a long way from equality: "While tasks take time, responsibility creates stress."

Use the influencing techniques in Chapter 11 to get other people in your family involved in sharing both tasks and a sense of responsibility about the cleanliness of the home, or making vacation arrangements, doctors' appointments, and so on.

Here's an inspiring example: My client Eileen, who works for a fashion company, took the 50% rule seriously and brought it into her family. She adapted the idea of the Ideal Day to the Ideal Home Life and led a discussion with her husband and two sons about the quality of life they wanted to experience at home. Her family members had a number of great ideas and helped out more than she thought they would! Each person took 10 minutes a day to clean a cluttered area of the house. After two weeks of every person doing their share, they felt their home had undergone a "makeover!" Each person made commitments about how to bring their own 50% to support a request that was important to each of the others. A totally fresh and positive dynamic took over the household!

Communicate so that you can manage others people's expectations and feel good about your choices. Once again, I turned to Jason Rubinstein to describe factors key to his successful balancing:

> Part of it is giving myself permission to shut off work, and on the other hand being able to actually permit myself to take some time on weeknights and weekends when needed. I've worked hard to build a strong enough relationship with my kids so they can understand in their 7 and 9-year-old brains that if I have to go into my office on a Sunday for a few hours, I am not leaving them. And before I went on a fully unplugged vacation, I over-communicated with everyone at work to make sure I had signed off on any open matters before I left.[16]

Recent surveys find that "young people" rated themselves as the most stressed of all the demographics.[17] And young people want/ demand work life conditions that are more balanced. Generation Y can lead their peers and all of us in naturally displaying the skills some of us may need to work toward developing. I asked Oi Yen Lam, MBA student of Duke's Fuqua Business school, how she handles her workload. Her strategies to thrive under stress include:[18]

- Keeping a sense of humor!
- Saying "no" to commitments where my participation is not crucial and/or lacks a definable goal/agenda.
- Adopting the 80/20 rule, and prioritizing activities with the biggest impact.
- Creating measurable, realistic goals. And, remembering it's OK if it's not perfect!
- Eating well, sleeping well, exercising regularly, and blocking out periods of "me" time on the calendar.
- Identifying mentors early on, and minimizing contact with "toxic" people.
- Recording my procrastination time, such as Facebook and online shopping, so I get a sense of how much time I am procrastinating— and this compels me to stop!

Can you see that her list shows she is already being impeccable for her 50%! You can too!

13

Call to Action:
Getting Others to Own Their 50%

"The best time to plant a tree was 20 years ago. The second best time is now."
—Chinese proverb

By now, can you appreciate that many people at home and at work may be on the Survival Under Stress cycle—but don't know it? As one participant in my training with Procter and Gamble said, playing on the drunk driving prevention slogan: "Friends don't let friends stay on the Survival Under Stress cycle!" Empathize with them; you may have been there too. And, just as any great mentor or parent, you can create a "teachable moment" by saying something like, "I used to push myself constantly. Then I started building in 'sprint-recovery time' and 'connect-the-dots time.'" Or encourage them: "Go Direct!" Recognize when they're telling "Stories" and guide them instead to act in the service of their Horizon Point. Remember that they are doing the best they can with the tools, the psychology and the biology they have.

The fastest way to improve the culture on a team, with your staff, or in your family is to create a "50% Culture" where everyone follows the 50% Rule: "Be impeccable for *your* 50%." Each person takes ownership of their contribution to the overall workings of the team or business.

Imagine for a moment that everyone you work with takes responsibility for doing their best: they do what you ask them to, communicate regularly and respond to you, use a respectful tone, and bring one another solutions, not problems. Your stress level is low and your productivity is off the charts! Ok, the alarm clock is ringing now, back to reality. . . .

But it doesn't have to be a dream.

Join me in my mission to create a "50% Culture" in your organization or business, in your family, in your community.

How can you do this?

1. Be an example.
2. Train your team or organization on these skills. When I facilitate team trainings we kick off with the "Ideal Day" exercise. We create a collective vision of an Ideal Day for the team. Then, each person makes commitments to contribute his or her part to create that day, every day. Once empowered, the team becomes high performing. They communicate to problem solve. They hold one another accountable using a positive tone.
3. If you have a blog, educate your readers about a 50% Culture. Give examples of how the 50% Rule works for you—and how it could work for them.
4. Introduce the 50% Rule in your community and volunteer group meetings, religious groups, or in professional associations. Encourage the people around the table to understand other points of view before getting stuck in their own.
5. Dream—big. Stress-induced behaviors were cannibalizing your energy reserves and holding you back. Now you can begin to make the contribution you were put here to make.

I challenge you: Take the 50% rule everywhere in your life. Hold yourself to this standard and overcome the daily stresses and obstacles that held you back—until today. You'll make an inner "fist pump" every time you walk away from reacting, every time you avoid getting caught up in the other person's 50%. You'll feel energized by your success when you Go Direct! And you'll enjoy the reserves of energy and enthusiasm you bring home at night because you found your "Off Button" during the day!

Practice the Success Under Stress techniques until they're second nature. Use the 50% rule to keep you at your Horizon Point—even when the temptation is to blame others, to feel overwhelmed, to keep pushing the On Button when you *know* you need the Off Button.

Don't be buried by stress. Surf the wave. And lift up the people around you. If each of us does our part, we can create a 50% culture in our families, communities, organizations and yes—even around the world. It starts with you.

The Top 12 Resilience Strategies
for Success Under Stress

The Golden Rule of Resilience to stress is be impeccable for your 50% in every situation. Here are 12 ways you can do that:

1. **Act in the service of your Horizon Point:** Instead of reacting to demands, impose control. Define the qualities/attributes of the person you want to be and make your daily purpose to act in the service of this endpoint (Chapter 3)

2. **Three-part breath:** This 3-minute exercise helps balance the energizing and calming parts of your nervous system and offers you a rapid mental reset (Chapter 4).

3. **Sprint-recovery pattern in your day:** A scheduling approach that allows you to maintain all day focus and energy by pushing yourself followed by a brief period of rejuvenation. Include exercise and breathing techniques as excellent "recovery" activities (Chapter 4).

4. **Eat right, sleep right:** Eat a low-sugar, high-protein diet to have long-lasting energy without dips throughout the day (Chapter 7).

Use Left Nostril Breathing to instantly calm you and help you get to sleep or put you back to sleep (Chapter 4).

5. **Cooling breath:** This breathing technique keeps you remain cool, calm, and collected instead of reactive in the face of other people's distress. It helps calm the other person down too (Chapter 10)!

6. **"Stories" log:** Learn to stop taking things personally by becoming more objective about other people's behavior and changing your "story" (Chapter 9).

7. **Go Direct!:** Learn to stop self imposing stress by building your own self-confidence rather than having to seek other people's approval or hold yourself back to prevent their disapproval (Chapter 6).

8. **A-C-T to eliminate most interruptions:** Take control over other people interrupting you by having preset criteria when you will accept, curtail, or triage interruptions (Chapter 5).

9. **Clarity is your best time-management tool:** Prioritize by having clarity on your role, a strategic objectives/business model, and high-value priorities. Then, be more intentional about saying "yes" and "no" to requests (Chapter 5).

10. **Panic Reset button:** Use the acupressure point to immediately reduce feelings of panic and anxiety (Chapter 7).

11. **F-I-R-E technique:** When someone else's behavior stresses you out, influence them by transferring the ownership with this four-step conversation technique (Chapter 11).

12. **Be the DJ of your mental iPod:** Change your self-critical and fearful self-talk with this technique (Chapter 8).

ENDNOTES

Introduction

1 Accenture. (2010, Mar.). Women Leaders and Resilience: Perspectives from the C-Suite, *Accenture Report*, p. 5.

2 Safian, R. (2012, Jan. 9). This Is Generation Flux: Meet the Pioneers of the New (and Chaotic) Frontier of Business. Retrieved from http://www.fastcompany .com/1802732/generation-flux-meet-pioneers-new-and-chaotic-frontier-business

Chapter 1

1 Hallowell, E. (2005). Overloaded Circuits: Why Smart People Underperform, *Harvard Business Review*, 3. Retrieved January 2005 from http://hbr.org/2005/01/ overloaded-circuits-why-smart-people-underperform/ar/1

2 Allen, D. (2012, Feb.) *Success Under Stress*, Interview with the Expert.

3 Cole, W. (2004, Oct. 11). Please, Go Away. *Time*. Retrieved October 2011 from http://www.time.com/time/magazine/article/0,9171,995299,00.html

4 American Psychological Association (2007, Oct. 24). Stress a Major Health Problem in the U.S., Warns APA. Retrieved October 2007 from http://www.apa.org/ news/press/releases/2007/10/stress.aspx

5 American Institute of Stress, from http://www.stress.org/americas.htm

Chapter 2

1   McEwen, B. (2002). *The End of Stress as We Know It*. Washington, DC: National Academies Press.

2   Anderson, C. (1977). The Relationship Between Locus of Control, Decision Behaviors, and Performance in a Stress Setting: A Longitudinal Study, *Academy of Management Proceedings, 00650668*, 65–69.

Chapter 3

1   Dyer, W. (1998). *Wisdom of the Ages: A Modern Master Brings Eternal Truths into Everyday Life*. New York: HarperCollins.

2   Amabile T., and Kramer, S. (2011). *The Progress Principle: Using Small Wins to Ignite Joy, Engagement, and Creativity at Work* (pp. 45–59). Boston: Harvard Business Press.

3   Zander, R. S., and Zander, B. (2003). *The Art of Possibility*. New York: Penguin.

4   Amabile and Kramer, *The Progress Principle*.

5   Seligman, M. (2011, Apr.). Building Resilience, *Harvard Business Review, 89*(4), 100–106.

6   Menkes, J. (2011). *Better Under Pressure: How Great Leaders Bring Out the Best in Themselves and Others*. Boston: Harvard Business Press.

7   Dweck, C. S. (2009). *Mindset, the New Psychology of Success*. New York: Ballantine Books.

8   Goldsmith, M. (2012, Feb.). New Finding Presented at Training for the American Management Association.

9   Barsh, J., Cranston, S., and Lewis, G. (2011). *How Remarkable Women Lead: The Breakthrough Model for Work and Life*. New York: Crown Business.

Chapter 4

1   Taylor, J. B. (2008). *My Stroke of Insight: A Brain Scientist's Personal Journey*. New York: Viking Press.

2   McEwan, B. (2002). *The End of Stress as We Know It*. Washington, DC: National Academies Press.

3   Rock, D. (2008). SCARF: A Brain-Based Model for Collaborating with and Influencing Others. *NeuroLeadership Journal, 1*(1), 296–320.

4   Angier, N. (2009, Aug. 18). Brain Is a Co-Conspirator in a Vicious Stress Loop. *The New York Times*, D2.

5   Schwartz, J., and Loehr, T. (2003). *The Power of Full Engagement: Managing Energy, Not Time, Is the Key to High Performance*. New York: Free Press.

6 Schwartz, T. (2011, Dec. 13). How to Accomplish More by Doing Less. Message posted to http://blogs.hbr.org

7 Schwartz, T. (2012, Feb.). *Success Under Stress*, Interview with the Expert.

8 Office Pulse, Work/Life Balance. (2011). *Captivate Office Pulse Survey Reveals Men Are Happier Than Women with Their Work–Life Balance.* Retrieved March 18, 2012 from http://officepulse.captivate.com/work-life-balance

9 Azar, B. (2000). A New Stress Paradigm for Women. Retrieved July 2000 from http://www.apa.org/monitor/julaug00/stress.aspx

10 Catalyst. (2005). Women "Take Care," Men "take charge": Stereotyping of U.S. Business Leaders Exposed. Retrieved March 18, 2012 from http://www.catalyst.org/publication/94/women-take-care-men-take-charge-stereotyping-of-us-business-leaders-exposed

11 Evans, C. (2012, Feb.). *Success Under Stress*, Interview with the Expert.

12 Schwartz, T. (2007, Oct.). Manage Your Energy, Not Your Time, *Harvard Business Review, 85.*

13 Knowledge at Wharton (2012). Flipping the Switch: Who Is Responsible for Getting Employees to Take a Break? Retrieved February 15, 2012 from http://knowledge.wharton.upenn.edu/article.cfm?articleid=2941

14 Kelly, C. (2012, Apr. 28). Ok, Google Take A Deep Breath, *The New York Times.* Retrieved from http://www.nytimes.com/2012/04/29/technology/google-course-asks-employees-to-take-a-deep-breath.html?

15 Berry, L, Mirabito, A., and Baun, W. (2010, Dec.). What's the Hard Return on Employee Wellness Programs? *Harvard Business Review, 88*(12), 105–112.

16 Sequeira, S. (2012, Feb.) *Success Under Stress*, Interview with the Expert.

17 Cromie, W.J. (2006, Feb. 2). Meditation Found to Increase Brain Size. *Harvard Gazette.*

18 Hölzel, B.K., Carmody, J., Evans, K.C., et al. (2010). Stress Reduction Correlates with Structural Changes in the Amygdala. *Social Cognitive and Affective Neuroscience, 5*(1), 11–17.

19 MacKenzie, C.S., Poulin, P.A., and Seidman-Carlson, R. (2006). A Brief Mindfulness-Based Stress Reduction Intervention for Nurses and Nurse Aides. *Applied Nursing Research, 19*, 105–109.

20 Kerr, C.E., Jones, S.R., Wan, Q., et al. (2011). Effects of Mindfulness Meditation training on Anticipatory Alpha Modulation in Primary Somatosensory Cortex. *Brain Research Bulletin, 85*(3–4), 96-103.

21 Kirk, U., Downar, J., and Montague, P.R. (2011). Interoception Drives Increased Rational Decision-Making in Meditators. Playing the Ultimatum Game. *Frontiers in Decision Neuroscience, 5*, 49.

22   Brown, R. P., and Gerberg, P.L. (2009). Yoga Breathing, Meditation, and Longevity. *Annals of the New York Academy of Sciences, 1172,* 54–62.

23   Levry, M. (2012, Feb.). *Success Under Stress,* Interview with the Expert.

24   Greene, G. (2012, Mar. 24). The Case for Sleep Medicine. *The New York Times.* Retrieved March 24, 2012 from http://www.nytimes.com/2012/03/25/opinion/sunday/the-case-for-sleep-medicine.html

25   Pick, M. (2011). Better Sleep May Lower Your Hunger Hormone. Retrieved February 4, 2011 from http://www.huffingtonpost.com

26   Weisul, K. (2011). So That's Why Your Boss Is Hypercritical. Retrieved August 4, 2011 from http://www.cbsnews.com

27   Gottfried, S. (2012, Feb.). *Success Under Stress,* Interview with the Expert.

28   Sequeira, S. (2012, Feb.). *Success Under Stress,* Interview with the Expert.

29   Schwartz, T. (2012, Feb.). *Success Under Stress,* Interview with the Expert.

30   Woods, W. (2012). Meditating at Work: A New Approach to Managing Work Overload. *Noetic Now, 19,* and Kelly, C. (2012, Apr. 28). Ok, Google Take a Deep Breath, *The New York Times.* Retrieved from http://www.nytimes.com/2012/04/29/technology/google-course-asks-employees-to-take-a-deep-breath.html?_r=1&pagewanted=all

31   Woods, Mediating at Work.

32   Davidson, R., Lutz, A., Lewis, J., and Johnstone, T. (2008). Regulation of the Neural circuitry of Emotion by Compassion Meditation. *PLoS ONE, 3*(3). doi: 10.1371/journal.pone.0001897

33   Rosenthal, N., and Oz, M. (2011). *Transcendence: Healing and Transformation Throught Transcendental Meditation.* New York: Penguin Group.

34   Winfrey, O. (2012, Feb.). What Oprah Knows for Sure About Finding the Fullest Expression of Yourself. Retrieved on February 2012 from http://http://www.oprah.com/health/Oprah-on-Stillness-and-Meditation-Oprah-Visits-Fairfield-Iowa

35   Schwartz, T. (2010). *The Way We're Working Isn't Working.* New York: Free Press.

36   Rock, D. (2009). *Your Brain at Work: Strategies for Overcoming Distraction, Regaining Focus, and Working Smarter All Day Long.* New York: HarperCollins.

37   Pick, M. (2011). *Are You Tired and Wired? Your Proven 30-Day Program for Overcoming Adrenal Fatigue and Feeling Fantastic Again.* New York: Hay House.

38   Gottfried, S. (2013). *The Hormone Cure: Reclaim Balance, Sleep, Sex Drive, and Vitality with the Gottfried Protocol.* New York: Scribner/Simon & Schuster.

Chapter 5

1   Obhi,S., and Haggard, P. (2004, July-Aug). Free Will and Free Won't. *American Scientist, 92*(4), 358–365.

2   Dolan, C. (2012, Feb.). *Success Under Stress,* Interview with the Expert.

3   Booz & Company. (2011). *Executives say They're Pulled in Too Many Directions and That Their Company's Capabilities Don't Support Their Strategy.* Retrieved January 18, 2011 from http://www.booz.com/global/home/press/article/49007867

4   McCaffrey, S. (2012, Feb.). *Success Under Stress,* Interview with the Expert.

5   Schefren, R. (2011). *From Frustration to Freedom Webinar.* http://www.livewebinar service.com/b/invitation.php

6   Dietzel, G. (2011). *The New Stealth Guru Webinar.* http://www.sellhighpriced programs.com/

7   Schefren, R. (2012, Feb.). *Success Under Stress,* Interview with the Expert.

8   Rock, D. (2009). *Your Brain at Work.* (pp. 93–95). New York: Harper Business.

9   Worline, M. (2012, Feb.). *Success Under Stress,* Interview with the Expert.

10 Cole, W. (2004, Oct. 11). "Please, Go Away." *Time.* Retrieved October 2011 from http://www.time.com/time/magazine/article/0,9171,995299.00.html

11 Traub, P. (2011, Nov.). Training for Women Presidents Organization, New York.

12 Knowledge at Wharton. (2012). *Flipping the Switch: Who Is Responsible for Getting Employees to Take a Break?* Retrieved February 15, 2012 from http://knowledge.wharton.upenn.edu/article.cfm?articleid=2941

13 Knowledge at Wharton, *Flipping the Switch.*

14 Dean, D., and Webb, C. (2011). Recovering from Information Overload. Retrieved March 18, 2012 from http://www.mckinseyquarterly.com/Recovering_from_information_overload_2735

15 Carr, N. (2010, June). *The Shallows: What the Internet Is Doing to Our Brains.* New York: W. W. Norton & Company.

16 Carr, N. (2011). Economist Conference: The Consequences of Information Overload. Video available at www.nicholascarr.com

17 Allen, D. (2002). *Getting Things Done: The Art of Stress-Free Productivity.* New York: Penguin Books.

18 Dux, P., Ivanoff, J., Asplund, C., and Marois, R. (2006). Isolation of a Central Bottleneck of Information Processing with Time-Resolved FMRI. *Neuron, 52,* 1109–1120.

19 Nigg, J. (2102, Mar.) *Success Under Stress,* Interview with the Expert.

20 Rock, D. (2009). *Your Brain at Work* (pp. 93-95). New York: Harper Business.

21 Morgan, C. (2012, Feb.). *Success Under Stress,* Interview with the Expert.

22 Knowledge at Wharton, *Flipping the Switch.*

23 Dolan, C. (2012, Feb.). *Success Under Stress,* Interview with the Expert.

24 Allen, *Getting Things Done.*

Section III Introduction

1   Clancy, R. (2010). *Financial Control Gives People More Happiness Than a Large Salary, Study Shows*. Retrieved March 18, 2012, from http:// www.investment international.com

Chapter 7

1   Ross, J. B. (2003). *The Mood Cure: The 4-Step Program to Take Charge of Your Emotions--Today*. New York: Penguin Books.

2   Gottfried, S. (2012, Feb.). *Success Under Stress,* Interview with the Expert.

3   Levry, J. M. (2012, Feb.). *Success Under Stress,* Interview with the Expert.

4   Sequeira, S. *Success Under Stress,* Interview with the Expert.

5   Wilson, J.L. (2001). *Adrenal Fatigue: The 21st Century Stress Syndrome*. Petaluma, CA: Smart Publications.

6   Gottfried, S. (2012, Feb.). *Success Under Stress,* Interview with the Expert.

7   Wilson, *Adrenal Fatigue*.

8   Pick, M. (2011). *Are You Tired and Wired? Your Proven 30-Day Program for Overcoming Adrenal Fatigue and Feeling Fantastic Again*. New York: Hay House, and Pick, M. (2012, Mar.). *Success Under Stress,* Interview with the Expert.

9   Ross, *The Mood Cure,* p. 73.

10   Ross, *The Mood Cure*.

11   Gottfried, *Success Under Stress,* Interview with the Expert.

12   Pick, *Are You Tired and Wired?* and *Success Under Stress,* Interview with the Expert.

Chapter 8

1   Goldsmith, M. (2007). *What Got You Here Won't Get you There: How Successful People Become Even More Successful!* New York, NY: Hyperion and www .marshallgoldsmithfeedforward.com

2   Fey, T. (2011). *Bossypants*. New York. Reagan Arthur Books.

3   Uzzi, B., and Dunlap, S. (2005). How to Build Your Network. *Harvard Business Review, 83*(12), 53–60.

Section IV Introduction

1   Watson, C., and Hoffman, R. (1996). Managers as Negotiators. *Leadership Quarterly, 7*(1), 1996. Retrieved from http://www.trainingindustry.com/uploadedFiles/ Executive_Toolkit/Knowledge_Community/White_Papers/Tracom_-_ Effective_Managers_WP.pdf

2   Weisul, K. (2011). How Office Stress Invades Our Homes. Retrieved September

6, 2011 from http://www.cbsnews.com/8301-505125_162-44442198/how-office-stress-invades-our-homes/

Chapter 9

1   Achor, S. (2010). *The Happiness Advantage: The Seven Principles of Positive Psychology That Fuel Success an Performance at Work.* New York: Crown Business.

2   Ferrazzi, K. (2009). *Who's Got Your Back: The Breakthrough Program to Build Deep, Trusting Relationships That Create Success – and Won't Let You Fail.* New York: Crown Business

Chapter 10

1   CBS Detroit. (2010). WSU Research Shows Husband's Work Worries Affect Wife's Hormones. Retrieved November 29, 2010 from http://detroit.cbslocal.com/2010/11/29/wsu-research-shows-husbands-work-worries-affect-wifes-hormones-2/

2   Taylor, J. B. (2008). *My Stroke of Insight: A Brain Scientist's Personal Journey.* New York: Viking Press.

3   Sequeira, S. (2012, Feb.). *Success Under Stress,* Interview with the Expert.

4   Levry, J. M. (2012, Feb.). *Success Under Stress,* Interview with the Expert.

5   Sequeira, *Success Under Stress,* Interview with the Expert.

6   Yates, B. (2012, Feb.). *Success Under Stress,* Interview with the Expert.

7   Emotional Freedom Techniques. (2011). The Effect of Emotional Freedom Techniques (EFT) on Stress Biochemistry: A Randomized Controlled Trial. Retrieved from http://www.eftuniverse.com/index.php?option=com_content&view=article&id=9160&Itemid=21

8   Childre, D., and Rozman, D. (2005). *Transforming Stress: The Heartmath Solution for Relieving Worry, Fatigue, and Tension.* Oakland, CA: New Harbinger Publications.

9   Davis, J. What's So Great About Kissing? *Webmd.com.* Retrieved from http://www.webmd.com/sex-relationships/features/kissing-benefits

10   Grewen K.M., Girdler S.S., Amico, J.A., and Light, K.C .(2005) . Effects of Partner Support on Resting Oxytocin, Cortisol, Norepinephrine and Blood Pressure Before and After Warm Partner Contact. *Psychosomatic Medicine, 67,* 531–538.

Chapter 11

1   Johnson, M. (2009). *Cracking The Boy's Club Code: The Woman's Guide to Being Heard and Valued in the Workplace.* New York: Morgan James Publishing.

2   Myers-Briggs. Myers-Briggs Type Indicator. Retrieved from https://www.cpp
    .com/products/mbti/index.aspx

3   Connell, H. (1984). NLP Techniques for Salespeople. *Mendeley, 38*(11), 44-46.
    Retrieved from http://www.mendeley.com/research/nlp-techniques-for-sales
    people/

4   Tracom Group. (2010). Journal Article Shows SOCIAL STYLE to Be Most Effec-
    tive Behavioral Model. Retrieved on November 9, 2010 from http://www.tracom
    corp.com/news-and-resources/news-detail.html?content_item_id=150

5   Ferrazzi, K. (2005). *Never Eat Alone: And Other Secrets to Success, One Relation-
    ship at a Time.* New York: Crown Business.

6   Dale Carnegie, as quoted in Ferrazzi, *Never Eat Alone.*

7   Guido, L. (2012, Feb.). *Success Under Stress,* Interview with the Expert.

Chapter 12

1   Families and Work Institute. (2002). 2002 National Study of the Changing Work-
    force. Retrieved from http://familiesandwork.org/site/work/workforce/ 2002nscw
    .html

2   Slaughter, A.-M. (2012). Why Women Still Can't Have it All. *The Atlantic Maga-
    zine,* July/August. Retrieved June 25, 2012 from http://www.theatlantic.com/
    magazine/archive/2012/07/why-women-still-cant-have-it-all/309020/

3   Rubinstein, J. (2012, Feb.). *Success Under Stress,* Interview with the Expert.

4   Kelly, M. (2011). *Off Balance: Getting Beyond the Work-Life Balance Myth to Per-
    sonal and Professional Satisfaction.* New York: Penguin Group

5   Evans, C. (2012, Jan.). *Success Under Stress,* Interview with the Expert.

6   Hansen, A. (2012, Feb.). *Success Under Stress,* Interview with the Expert.

7   Ferrazzi, K. (2005). *Never Eat Alone: And Other Secrets to Success, One Relation-
    ship at a Time.* New York: Crown Business

8   Evans, C. (2012, Jan.). *Success Under Stress,* Interview with the Expert.

9   Evans, C. (2012, Jan.). *Success Under Stress,* Interview with the Expert.

10   Moen, P., Kelly, E.L., Tranby, E., and Huang, Q. (2011). Changing Work, Chang-
    ing Health: Can Real Work-Time Flexibility Promote Health Behaviors and
    Well-Being? *Journal of Health and Social Behavior, 52*(4), 404–429.

11   Alphonse, L.M. (2012). Working Mothers Are Healthier (STUDY). Retrieved
    January 3, 2012 from http://shine.yahoo.com/work-money/working-mothers-
    healthier-study-220400211.html

12   Williams, J. (2011). One Third of Employees Willing to Change Employer for
    Flexible Working Arrangements. Computerweekly.com. Retrieved August 23

2011 from http://www.computerweekly.com/news/2240105418/One-third-of-employees-willing-to-change-employer-for-flexible-working-arrangements

13 Evans, *Success Under Stress,* Interview with the Expert.

14 Working Mother's Research Institute. (2011) What Moms Choose: The Working Mother Report. Retrieved from http://www.workingmother.com/research-institute/what-moms-choose-working-mother-report

15 Evans, *Success Under Stress,* Interview with the Expert

16 Rubinstein, *Success Under Stress,* Interview with the Expert.

17 Cohen, S., and Janicki-Deverts, D. (2012, June). Who's Stressed? Distributions of Psychological Stress in the United States in Probability Samples from 1983, 2006, and 2009. *Journal of Applied Social Psychology, 42*(6), 1320–1334.

18 Lam, O.Y. (2011, Feb.). *Success Under Stress*, Interview with the Expert.

INDEX

sense of purpose and, 35, 39, 83
stories and, 168–169
Hormones, stress, 53, 68, 136–138.
See also Cortisol
Hugging, kissing and, 186–187
Huxley, Aldous, 19

I

Ideal Day exercise, 28–29, 219
Ideal Home Life, 216
Illness and disease, 137, 182
Implication, 198–199, 201
Indirect Path behavior, 120–121
concerns of, 125
Direct Path behavior compared
to, 123–124, 128–129
false confidence from, 121
feedback and boomerang effect
of, 127
throwing you off track through,
121
wasted time from, 120
wasting energy with, 121
Individual responsibility, 45
Influencing people, 78, 189–207,
216
action plan for, 206
with customize communications
to cut through resistance,
194–197
four principles for, 190–205
with lead with generosity to
create bigger game, 203–205
Match Before Move for, 202–203
points to remember for, 206–207
resources for, 207
for their reasons, not yours,
190–194

with transfer ownership of
problem, 197–203
WIIFT and, 191–194, 198–200
Inform yourself, but don't obsess,
154
Inner pharmacy, xx, 133
Inner work life
control of, 34
positive compared to negative, 46
Innovation and creativity, 99–100
Inspirational or emotional appeal,
196–197
Instant Bliss exercise, 69
Institute of Heartmath, 186
Integrate worlds, 214
Intention
with availability, 96, 98–99
control and, 34–35
thinking in service of, 34
Interruptions
accept or allow, 94
A-C-T on, 94–98, 222
cut it off at the pass (or curtail),
94–95
eliminating, 32, 59
number of daily, 93
triage, 95–96
Intuition
access to, 52–53, 57, 135
gut instincts and, 135–136, 148
Intuition Log, 147–148, 152

J

Judgment, validated, 148

K

Kegan, Robert, 93
Kelley, Matthew, 212

ABOUT THE AUTHOR

Sharon Melnick, PhD, is a business psychologist whose passion for teaching stress resilience tools fuels leaders and business owners to break out of the pack and get results in times of flux. Her practical behavior change tools are informed by 10 years of research at Harvard Medical School, field tested by more than 6,000 training participants, and applied by hundreds of clients to succeed at their next level.

As CEO of Horizon Point Inc., she has successfully coached high potentials, senior executives, and sales professionals at companies such as Deutsche Bank, Oracle Corporation, Freddie Mac, Pitney Bowes, and Deloitte, as well as solo entrepreneurs and owners of small companies. Her trainings on resilience, influence, and leadership under stress have been sought after for high-potential emerging leaders, women leaders, and multicultural leaders at companies both in the United States and abroad, such as GE, Procter & Gamble, Bloomberg, Pfizer, Merck, and Coldwell Banker. Her presentations receive the highest ratings and repeat invitations from organizations such as the American Management Association, the National Association of Female Executives, Working Mother Media, Women in Cable and Telecommunications, Women Presidents Organization, Rainmakers Forum, and the Healthcare Businesswomen's Association. Discover her online programs and downloadable mobile applications at www.sharonmelnick.com